A LAND OF GODS AND GIANTS

Nine Stone Close stone circle and Robin Hood's Stride, Birchover, Derbyshire.

A LAND OF GODS AND GIANTS

MICK SHARP

INTRODUCTION BY CHRISTOPHER CHIPPINDALE

ALAN SUTTON
1989

ALAN SUTTON PUBLISHING
BRUNSWICK ROAD · GLOUCESTER · UK

ALAN SUTTON PUBLISHING INC
WOLFEBORO · NEW HAMPSHIRE · USA

First published 1989

British Library Cataloguing in Publication Data

Sharp, Mick *1952–*
A land of gods and giants.
1. Great Britain. Prehistoric antiquities
I. Title
936.1'01

ISBN 0-86299-664-3

Library of Congress Cataloging in Publication Data
applied for

The Introduction is for Charlie

Front cover. The Stones of Stennes, Orkney
Back cover. Mulfra Quoit, West Penwith, Cornwall

Designed by Richard Bryant and Martin Latham
Cover Design   Martin Latham
Typesetting and origination by Alan Sutton Publishing Limited
Colour origination by J-Film Processing Ltd, London
Printed by New Inter Litho in Italy

PREFACE

Were it not for a few stone walls which intervene in the foreground, the solitude of the place and the boundless views are such as almost carry the observer back through the multitude of centuries and make him believe that he sees the same view and the same state of things as existed in the days of the architects of this once holy place.

Thus wrote Thomas Bateman in 1848, in his *Vestiges of the Antiquities of Derbyshire*, of Arbor Low on Middleton Moor.

Coming from Derby, it was natural that family trips to the Peak District formed part of my boyhood, and should include visits to such ancient sites as Stanton Moor and Arbor Low. The appearance and atmosphere of these places made a strong impression on me, and so, unwittingly, my parents set me on a course which has perplexed them ever since.

On these early visits to Arbor Low, I noted its looming bank of earth, rising from a slope of pasture, and enclosing a circular ditch. Entrances through the bank on the NNW and SSE led, via causeways across the ditch, to a grassy platform bearing fifty or so large slabs of limestone lying prostrate. It had majesty. It had power. It felt familiar. It made sense.

I now know that Arbor Low is one of the best preserved examples of a class II 'henge' monument, built in the period of transition between the Late Neolithic and Early Bronze Age, about four thousand years ago. This type of monument is found all over Britain, but not elsewhere, and the central area can be empty or bear arrangements of stones, wooden posts, pits and burials. They are believed to have been used for ceremonial and inter-tribal activities such as stone axe trading.

This is interesting, but not very satisfying, and I have returned time and again to Arbor Low, drawn not by this knowledge, but by my original intuitive recognition that it is a special place.

It took a long time, but finally I managed to make a photograph of Arbor Low which contains some of the qualities of the place which effect me so much. It is on page 91 and I will let it speak for itself.

After training as an industrial photographer, three years at art college allowed me to start bringing together, through the medium of photography, my love of the British landscape, a fascination with prehistoric beliefs and practices, an appreciation of natural forms as sculpture and mirrors of psychological states, and my innate need, shared with many other people, to create and visit sacred places.

The sites which particularly interest me, and feature in this book, are those with a presumed ceremonial or 'ritual' dimension; causewayed camps, megalithic tombs, earthen barrows, henges, stone circles, standing stones, and rock carvings, made and used in the Neolithic and Bronze Age between around 4500 and 800 BC.

Because of their inherent romance, they have long attracted the attention of artists, antiquarians, poets and mystics, and the anonymous weavers of folktale and myth, burdened with an overwhelming desire to explain, and tell a good story.

The rather unbalanced, and, at times, positively lunatic view of prehistory which can result from a study of such remains in isolation, is gradually being filled out as archaeologists learn to recognise and interpret the more perishable remains of the past, and begin to fit 'ritual' sites into the context of the communities and societies which made and used them.

In the 'Lowland Zone' of the south and east, many of the upstanding monuments of earth, wood and stone have been cleared away. They reveal their presence, and some of their secrets, only to those with knowledgeable eyes, in certain conditions of weather, plant growth and light, or to the insistent probings of archaeological excavation with its growing array of scientific techniques.

In the 'Highland Zone' of the west and north, in a broad diagonal sweep from Cornwall to Shetland, the earth and stone monuments have better survived the onslaught of time, weather and the changing needs and fears of society. Their dramatic and austere forms are still to be seen in abundance, set against the ever changing background of sky and season. With notable exceptions, such as the remarkable area around Avebury in Wiltshire, and the Medway in Kent, it is the sites and landscapes of the west and north which have drawn me, and feature most prominently in this book.

As this is a personal selection, based on photographic considerations rather than archaeological ones, there are many omissions, and to those who cannot find their favourite sites here, I apologise.

I make no apology, however, for not including Stonehenge. To me it has always seemed atypical, ugly, and disappointing to visit, having none of the raw power and beauty of humbler, less well known sites. Stonehenge is a dead thing, with all the bad qualities of sophistication – the worst kind of 'public monument' – strangled by officialdom and neutered by bad taste. Stonehenge may once have been a special place, it may be again, but it isn't now.

For me, many prehistoric sites are special places imbued with a sense of otherness and accumulated sanctity. They still have meaning and significance in a time that is trying to render such things irrelevant, and they retain an atmosphere and power capable of provoking a strong response.

When studied with care and understanding, all the remains of prehistory have their fascination and interest, but it is the stones and their interaction with the landscape which capture and hold the imagination. This is, unashamedly, what I have tried to do with my photographs.

To Jean for having to live for the future while I lived in the past.

CONTENTS

Ballymeanoch standing stones,
Kilmartin Valley, Argyll.

POWER

Quoyness chambered cairn, Sanday, Orkney.

BURIAL

Bryn Celli Ddu passage grave and henge, Anglesey, Gwynedd.

SACRED AREAS

Callanish I stone circle and passage grave, Isle of Lewis, Outer Hebrides.

SYMBOLS AND IMAGES

Achnabreck rock carvings, Lochgilphead, Argyll.

ANCIENT STONES IN CHANGING LANDSCAPES

The King Stone, Rollright, Oxfordshire.

INTRODUCTION

The pictures in this book require no explanation. They speak for themselves in their own language of images; the photographer himself says what else he wishes in their captions. Instead, in this introductory essay, I try to set out why it is important to see the ancient places of our land of gods and giants in the way this book sees them, with a vision that is dramatic and magical, as well as by the cooler eye of analytical science.

1

When topographers and antiquarians began to explore and excavate the ancient sites and burial mounds of Britain, they were not the first to notice these old places. The mounds had been given names, both general and particular, a thousand years before. In much of England they were called 'barrows', a word deriving from the Anglo-Saxon word *beorh*. In the southwest they were 'touts', in the north of England 'lows', again from an Anglo-Saxon word. Many of the burial mounds had individual names known to countrymen; names like Black Barrow or Sandy Barrow for their colour or construction, or names for the stories that went with them, Robin's Barrow or Robin Hood's Butts from tales of Robin Hood, or Wayland's Smithy from its story of a blacksmith's forge.

Many of those names refer to giants, a Giant's Barrow in Hampshire, Giants' Caves in Wiltshire and Giants' Hills in Lincolnshire, a Giant's Quoit in Cornwall, and more than a dozen Giant's Graves in counties from Cornwall to Shetland. Barclodiad-y-Gawres, 'the apronful of the giantess', is a giant monument named in Welsh. The Giant's Graves are, for the most part, the elongated mounds, 10 feet high, 20 or 30 feet wide and 60 or 100 feet long, that are rarer and, we now know, much older than the common round barrows. The Saxons had noticed the difference, too; the *langan hlaew* mentioned in the Saxon bounds of Tackley, Oxfordshire, had become 'Long Banck' on a map of 1605, and was perfectly recognizable as a long barrow on the ground in 1930. As the burial of a man leaves a hump in the ground, a foot high, 2 or 3 feet wide and 7 or 8 feet long, so should a giant not make a giant hump? – the more so when the profile of the mound, like West Kennet in Wiltshire, undulates as it might over the knees and feet of an outsized corpse. In north Holland there were similar mounds, with rude stone tables set within them, and they have similar names. Patrick, patron saint of Ireland, raised a dead giant from his stony grave in a celebrated story:

> And Patrick came to Dichuil to a great grave, of astounding breadth and prodigious length which his familia had found. And with great amazement they marvelled that it extended 120 feet, and they said: 'We do not believe this affair, that there was a man of this length.' And Patrick answered and said: 'If you wish you shall see him.' And they said 'We do.' And he struck with his crozier a stone near his head and signed the grave with the sign of cross, and said: 'Open, O lord, the grave.' And the holy man opened the earth and the giant arose whole, and said: 'Blessed be you, O holy man, for you have raised me even for one hour from many pains.'

The giant could not be permitted to walk abroad, for men could not look upon his face for fear. Baptized by the saint and confessing God, he fell silent and was placed once more down into his grave.

With the giant building slabs of rough stone and with the giant size of the long mounds went other stories of the giants who had built and still protected them. The giant who built the Quoit at Zennor had made it immovable; whosoever might shift the stones would find they returned of their own accord. Near the Giant's Grave at Melcombe Horsey in Dorset were two stones, thrown by the giants, which move when they hear the cock crow at Cheselbourne.

Sometimes there were even found the bones of the giants themselves: a skeleton of 'gigantick stature' near Flowers Barrow in Dorset, the bones of an 'excessively big carcase' in a long vault under a Cornish barrow that was opened before 1600. A crofter who emptied the skeleton from an old stone grave in North Uist, Outer Hebrides, found its skull to be 'so vast that when placed on his own head it covered his shoulders'. The man had no sleep until he had reburied the bones in a proper peace.

2

Victorian researchers, medically trained and following the 19th-century fascination with skulls and their measurement, pursued the ancient skeletons out of the graves, examined them and swiftly abolished the stories. Dr John Thurnam excavated 22 of the Wiltshire long barrows altogether. There were no giants, although there were many fine crania, of a good size and distinctive elongated shape, to be illustrated with minute and affectionate detail in the engravings of his large book *Crania Britannica*.

Thomas Bateman, digging the barrows of the Peak district, took local advice; 'the natives' told him that the name of a barrow near Ecton was 'The Comp'. But it was the surer evidence of excavation that told him on 6 May 1848 the reality of its contents, the calcined remains of an adult accompanied by a bone pin and a spearhead of flint, and the unburnt skeleton of a very young child – both of them, as the rational and modern researcher knew to expect, beings of a perfectly ordinary stature.

With the giant's stories there also faded away the other tales, of saints in golden coffins, of Devil's Stones and Humps which Satan had built, of fairies who made mid-day music at the barrows, of King Arthur waiting under a barrow with his sleeping warriors, and most famously – from its recounting in both *Beowulf* and in the *Mabinogion* – of a great treasure in a secret passage under a mound that was guarded by a dragon. Bateman explained, of his ten years' researches in the 1850s:

> All written or traditional literature except the Hebrew Scripture and the oldest portion of the Vedes, being either so late as to possess little authority, or so much overlaid with myth and fable as to be inextricably confused and contradictory, so that we gladly recur to the buried treasures, and as the geologist re-peoples our planet from fossil remnants of the fauna and flora of its successive strata, each group presenting characters by which it may be distinguished from all others, so we exhume materials for the reconstruction, or rather for the elucidation of the history of mankind, a theme of all purely scientific subjects the most interesting, and only of late arrived at the importance it deserves.

3

For a century and a half, then, the myths and fables of ignorant old country folk have fallen before the surer testimony of scientific evidence. In this century the spade gave way to the more delicate mason's trowel, and now is helped by a growing armoury of techniques from the physical sciences. When Colt Hoare dug Wiltshire barrows during the years of the Napoleonic wars, he left the skulls behind, out of a respect for the dead and because there was nothing to be done with them. Now we have many things to do with the bones. We take those from a recent excavation, like the Hazleton long mound in Gloucestershire, crunch up little samples and treat them with fearsome chemicals, convert them to a smear of elemental carbon on a metal disc, place the smear in a perfect vacuum, and zap it by some awesome voltage of electricity, single atom by single atom, in a mass spectrometer in a north Oxford basement. The result is an exact radiocarbon determination, which some statistical magic – in turn dependent on varying cosmic ray flux from the sun – converts to an age of death, plus or minus a few score years, for that human being whose bones we have fried. Where Colt Hoare and Bateman knew these bones only as coming from some era beyond the present age, we know that the human femur from the Hazleton north entrance dates to 4760±60 'radiocarbon years before present'. This, by the mystery of science, is not at all the same thing as saying it is 4760 years old. It is equivalent to 3650 BC, more or less, about five and a half thousand years old. It makes him a thousand years older than the builders of the Egyptian pyramids.

This is just the start. In those bones is DNA; when the new genetic wizards learn better how to extract it and analyse it, we shall be able to look into his chromosomes and tell, perhaps, his blood group or see the colour of his long-dead eyes.

So far, so good. A flood of light, of scientific understanding illuminates the prehistory and early history of Britain. We know that standing stones do not at night go down to the water to drink. We know that flint arrowheads are flint arrowheads, not elf-bolts, and we know rather precisely the dates of their different distinctive shapes. If new Australian research is correct in finding traces of ancient blood on flint artefacts and identifying the blood to species, we shall know if the arrowheads were actually shot into bodies, and if into bodies, whether into the bodies of people or of deer.

4

Yet the gaining of this knowledge – scientific, reliable, secure, objective, testable, sceptical – comes at a cost. It is a limited kind of material knowledge, gained by the evidence of those physical objects themselves which – by definition – are all the evidence we have from remote prehistoric times. As we have gained that knowledge, so we have lost the personal stories, the vivid tales of individual, named human and superhuman beings.

Take the ancient site of Wayland's Smithy, on the old Ridgeway path in Oxfordshire, that now lies peacefully in a dark copse of beeches. It is a long mound – a giant's grave – with a stone chamber. Its name comes from folk story:

> At this place lived formerly an invisible Smith; and if a traveller's Horse had lost a Shoe upon the road, he had no more to do, than to bring the Horse to this place, with a piece of money, and leaving both there for some little time, he might come again and find the money gone, but the Horse new shod.

The name of Wayland occurs in Saxon legend; Wayland, son of the giant Wade, was apprenticed to the trolls who, like the elves, practised their magical metal crafts during the night at forges hidden in barrows and mounds.

So similar are the legends of German and Danish mythology to the English story of Wayland's Smithy that one can be sure that it was Saxon settlers in the country who brought the tale with them and re-made it for this mound in their new land. It has nothing to do with the mound's builders. But why did they choose this particular mound? Archaeology gives one answer, in the iron currency-bars or ingots found beneath a stone of the Smithy in 1919. The bars date to perhaps 50 BC, several centuries before the Saxon incursion, but perhaps others were found in Saxon times, and brought the story to the mound.

But suppose the story is not Saxon; despite so many coincidences, it *might* be older and genuinely of the place. Then archaeology still offers a certainty that the Smithy had nothing to do with smiths, for the mound and its stone chamber (and the wooden chamber that preceded it in an earlier stage) are demonstrably Neolithic in date, from an era many centuries before the working of iron or any other metal in England. No story of metal and smiths can have anything genuinely to do with its building.

The simplest, and the most important, of all the transformations in our knowledge of ancient Britain that has come from more than a century of scientific archaeology is our appreciation of the time-depth of human settlement. Those first farmers – the builders of sites like Wayland's Smithy – are now known to have come into England and Ireland at some date near 4500 BC. Sir Richard Colt Hoare set the Wiltshire barrow-builders as having preceded by a few centuries the Roman occupation of Britain in AD 43. Stuart Piggott's 1954 study of Neolithic Britain placed the farmers' arrival near 2000 BC; and now we push them beyond 4000 BC. So the builders of the long mounds are distanced from us by 6000 years; they are twice as remote from the Romano-British than we are from Julius Caesar. Straight away, we can see that folk legends that run back to Saxon times – or, with luck, even so very far as the Celts or Druids of the time of the Roman conquest – are in no sense original to the really ancient places like Wayland's Smithy or Callanish, the sites that are the subject of this book.

To be sure, the sites of later prehistory are more accessible, and sometimes even touch on the details of recorded history. Mortimer Wheeler excavated the hill-fort of Maiden Castle in Dorset with the Latin histories of the conquest of Britain for a guide, knew the tribal name of its defenders to be the Durotriges, and identified mass graves as the soldiers' burials. He knew that modern Dorchester, in the valley below, was the Roman centre that took the hill-fort's place. But there is a Neolithic long mound, date perhaps 4000 BC, that also runs across the hill-top. It was built, abandoned, eroded – and, surely, forgotten – many centuries before the defences of Maiden Castle were set around what must have seemed a virgin site in the Iron Age, over three thousand years later. So was the great circle of immense oak posts, whole tree-trunks probably, which runs under the Roman and the modern town of Dorchester and is, again, of Neolithic date. Even if we can try to grasp what it was to be Roman, citizen of an earlier federated Europe, how can one comprehend that world which is four thousand years further away and twice as remote in all aspects?

As our knowledge of the early farmers' sites has increased, so has our perplexity. There are a very few scrappy remains of little rectangular houses, and the farmers' work is revealed also by the pollen of cereals and arable-land weeds. But for the most part the sites are grand and of no simple or obvious function: long mounds, far larger than is required to decently cover the largest corpse; 'cursuses', long parallel pairs of banks and ditches that run across country, of unknown purpose and meaning; round enclosures of two types – first 'causewayed camps', then 'henges' – which have banks and ditches, often on the grandest scale, but the ditches have many gaps or the ditch is on the inside, where it gives no defensive advantage; stones set upright, singly, in pairs, in rings. There is burial but not of a respectable and christian kind. There is evidence of the oddest things being done with bones; corpses are left outdoors to lose their flesh before the larger bits are buried; heads are separated from the long bones; long bones are sorted into different types. There is evidence of trade and exchange, or at least of the moving of polished stone and flint axes about the islands, but the axes do not follow the plain logic of economical distribution, with each axe factory serving its local region. No, the axes travel right across the country, even two or three hundred miles into the very neighbourhoods where other outcrops are the quarry-sites for equally fine axes.

5

Near Brandon, on the Norfolk–Suffolk border, is Grimes Graves, an area of chalkland pocked by the holes and hummocks of Neolithic mines, where the fine flint was quarried to make those polished axes. And in Brandon itself, there was into this century a famous local industry of flint-knapping, not for axes by then, but making the little gun-flints, of exact shapes, which are used in early firearms. (They are still in some demand by gun-collectors.) The Brandon knappers seemed heirs to those troglodyte ancestors who had quarried the same seams and understood in the same way and by the same instincts the skills and quirks of making the flint break to shape. Knappers had been on the heaths of Brandon since time, if not immemorial, at least for some 4000 years. Tyro archaeologists like Louis Leakey, as a young Cambridge researcher who would make his name by fabulous discoveries in east Africa, made the pilgrimage to Brandon to see the knappers at their antique craft. Yet a recent study of the written sources for Brandon history shows that gunflint-knapping was a craft which only came to the town in the 18th century at earliest. It was very few centuries old when the last knappers gave up the business;

gnarled and rustic they may have been, and evocative their trade of primeval time, but they were no Neolithic survivors.

While the date of the great monuments of early Britain has been moving back, we have moved forward, from the mid years of the 19th century to, soon, the fringe of the 21st. In technology and in society there has been more change in these decades that in any previous era – all of it in a manner calculated to take us into a way of life which has lost almost all resemblance to that of the prehistoric people of these islands. We are vastly knowledgeable about every aspect of the material world, and vastly logical, at least in theory, in how we address it. Our children see every day that meat comes in plastic packs from supermarkets, milk in glass from the electric float. We regret that they do not know a traditional working farmyard. But consider how recent is that 'traditional working farmyard' or 'common-sense' knowledge, even in those country matters which ought, surely, to be shared with the peasant farmers of Neolithic Britain. They, too, had sheep and cattle and pigs; they, too, grew wheat and barley. Take for instance, the making of cider – not the gassy sweet stuff that was invented in factories, but real farmhouse scrumpy, made by a more natural fermentation. That must go back for ever! The fermenting of apples presumably does, but for any insight into how fermenting worked, of why it is that some brews of scrumpy go well, while some turn nasty or will not go at all, and for a few simple rules-of-thumb that improve the brewing, one can find no earlier guides than the study which Abraham Crocker published in the west country during the closing years of the 18th century. Indeed, most of the apparatus of 'traditional agriculture', its careful rotations, its drainage schemes, its programmes of stock breeding and selection, its principles of good husbandry, is not traditional at all, but a self-consciously modern product of Crocker's time, that age of reasoned agricultural improvement when a scientific agriculture began.

The world as the medieval peasant experienced it – with its darkness and sorcery, its illiteracy and ill-health, its ignorance and squalor – is surely beyond our real comprehension. How profound was the medieval ignorance of the plainest facts of chemistry or medicine. And how much more remote and bizarre is the Neolithic, when the most simple and 'obvious' logic of everyday life, the links between food and health, or between sexual relations and pregnancy, or between pregnancy and birth, may well have wholly escaped human understanding.

6

In these several ways, then, we are separated from the people who built the stone rings and the megalithic cairns, or quarried the ditches of the henges; much more separated by the strange circumstances of late twentieth-century life than those very few people who took an interest two centuries ago thought themselves to be. This must, I think, further reduce our chances of grasping the essence of the old sites. Yet there are other changes in our knowledge of ancient Britain which may bring us closer.

Most striking of these is our understanding of the changing natural history of the British Isles. Another 'obvious' division, the one between a static natural world, studied by biologists, and a changing human world, studied by historians, is a recent one – so recent in fact that the making of the division is still in its final stages. It is only this year that the famous London museum of natural history in South Kensington becomes, officially, the 'Natural History Museum'; until now it has legally been the 'British Museum (Natural History)', a title that is a relic of the 19th-century split of the old, undivided British Museum into two collections, one for dead people who have history and art, one for dead creatures of other kinds who have biology and instinct. Yet the natural world is not static; plants, especially, have been studied with such care and so long now that they can be seen to be changing, century by century, in their preferred habitats, and even in their characteristic features. Some taxonomies of the classic Linnean scheme are beginning to lose their accuracy, as the plants have sufficiently changed in the two centuries or so since the species and sub-species were defined that the distinguishing features no longer neatly divide them.

And plants do not, in Britain, live in isolation from human beings, whose impact on the landscape – by cutting, burning, ploughing, grazing, draining, building – has been overwhelming for centuries. If a 'natural landscape' is one whose parent state is unaffected by the human presence, then there are no natural landscapes in the British Isles, or perhaps in Europe as a whole. Everywhere, high and low, has felt many centuries of human interference.

The most characteristic British landscapes have an artificial aspect without being wholly human artefacts, for the living creatures do not always do as they are told. The chalk grassland of the English downs, for example, is the result of a particular rural way of human life, with a special place for sheep-grazing, that goes back to medieval times and beyond. The chalkland flora and fauna has grown to live with the sheep, and it is that particular rural regime that has kept the downs as grassland. In the post-war years, the rural regime has changed as almost all the grassland has been ploughed up for, especially, the growing of corn. The grassland flora and fauna has dwindled. The conservation societies who have rescued fragments of the 'traditional' chalkland find they have to cut and clear the hawthorn scrub that constantly invades and makes it 'tumble back' to woodland. Left to itself, and protected from grazing animals, almost any patch of Britain will turn itself to wood; when the experiment was tried in 1882, Broadbalk Wilderness in Hertfordshire changed itself from an arable field in 1882 to a wood in 1914. The old grassland is in large part the artificial product of a particular way humans have chosen to treat the chalk. And in Dorset and Wiltshire there can sometimes be seen under that ancient grassland the traces of ancient square 'Celtic fields', relics of an earlier time in prehistory when the downs were previously under the plough. The reforms of European agricultural policy now in progress may swing the pendulum once more, with the tide of cereals receding from the higher downs, and grazing or abandonment to waste will make another return.

Here, in the natural and artificial aspects of the landscape, is a most inviting way to grasp Neolithic realities. The ancient woods of England, for example, are not the surviving fragments of the first forest, the 'wildwood' that spread across the islands after the Ice-age glaciers retreated. Rather, places like Hayley Wood in Cambridgeshire and Bradfield Woods in Suffolk are of natural origin, but they have been managed since early medieval times. Most often they have been coppiced. Young trunks are cut and used especially for firewood; the stump sends up new shoots which in a dozen or score of years are cut again. The big 'stools' in ancient woodland may be many hundreds of years old, although the stems that grow from them this year are of the 1980s; those old stools are probably the most ancient living things in Britain. There is ample evidence — from the plants themselves, from place-names, charters and Domesday book, and from the earth banks and ditches round woods — that many of these woods have been cut and husbanded for a thousand years. And from the Neolithic peatlands of the Somerset Levels, one of the few regions of Britain where waterlogged sediment has preserved the perishable artefacts of the first farmers, there has come evidence of coppicing. Among the trackways making dry routes across the marsh is the Sweet Track that runs straight across the Levels for nearly 2 km; its date of 4000 BC makes it the oldest built road in the world. Its rods and planks show evidence of having grown in coppice; hazel and ashwood pegs that hold the track together come from coppice as well. A little younger is the Walton Heath track, which is built of hurdles. The Walton hurdles were woven of hazel rods from coppice and to much the same pattern as hurdles are made in the Levels today. So here is evidence of coppicing, in the medieval manner, that runs back six thousand years. A skilled and informed choice of different woods, ash and oak and hazel, for different parts of the trackways shows that the Neolithic track-builders had an equally good craft knowledge of the character of each kind of timber.

In short, the Somerset Levels show evidence of woodland *management* right back in the Neolithic of 6000 years ago, not just random cutting from a wildwood but the patterned exploitation of a renewable resource in a manner which puts to shame our greedy burning-up of unrenewable resources. But notice the word 'management', a thoroughly modern concept if ever there was one. There are good scientific reasons, to do with the physical strengths and structures of different timbers, why hazel is good for some purposes, ash for others, elm for yet others. Self-consciously rational ourselves, we find rationality in prehistoric people who 'managed' their landscape, and 'invested' in the good order of its 'planned' woodlands. But did they manage as a 20th-century businessman does? Did they even 'husband' as a good husbandman did, in the older country phrase? Did they choose hazel because it was recommended as the prehistoric consumer's best buy?

As for timber, so with other materials. Archaeologists have laid trackways, built round-houses, made flint axes and cut down trees with them, found how effective and elegant a tool is the lighter metal axe of the Bronze Age, ploughed, sown and harvested, and kept the harvest grain overwintering in storage pits. With that direct experience has come a growing respect for the craft skills and knowledge of Britain's first farmers. Some crafts, like the moving and setting-up of great stones, are harder to comprehend, but they can be replicated also. By analysing the age and sex of domestic animal bones, zoo-archaeologists have determined whether herds or flocks were kept for meat or wool or milk, because each has its characteristic killing pattern. And there is a mass of very detailed information about the environment where people lived. Insect carapaces and preserved fungi indicate just how wet the Somerset wetlands were. Snail shells preserved in soil profiles map the changes over time in the balance of chalkland vegetation. Flying ants in the stacked turves at the centre of Silbury Hill prove that the building of this, the greatest prehistoric mound of Europe, began in those few August days when the ants come out to fly.

These studies have great strength precisely *because* they depend very little on what prehistoric people believed their lives were about. We have no understanding of what the Neolithic track-builders saw themselves as doing. The economical logic of their work is clear to us, the making of dry routes running by the short routes from one place to another, and we are comfortable if we identify an economic motive, efficiency from point to point, as the idea of it all. We know just when Silbury Hill was built, to the century by radiocarbon, and within that century almost to the precise day of the year, but when it comes to *why* it was built or *what* it stands for, we offer only shadowy abstractions.

We see no spirits in the woods, no gods in the trees, no sprites in the branches, no fairies in the clearings. We may regret the cutting of trees because it reduces vegetational diversity, amenity value or recreational opportunities, but not for any matter of the spirit beyond a vague respect for things green.

It is this which sets us moderns apart. The inhabitants of Britain, in all previous recorded generations, were believing people, and among the lesser things they believed in were those stories of ancient times and ancient places, the folk tales whose truth is lost to us.

7

For me, there is one simple means that helps in taking oneself from the modern to the ancient place. This is walk to the site. We know nothing about the mood or spirit with which prehistoric people came to the stone rings at Stanton Drew or Arbor Low, whether they were the women or the children or the strong or all three, whether they did it by daylight or by moonshine, in joy or in fear. We do know they came on foot (and on their own feet; no domestic horses until a later period). To arrive by foot, in modern dress, is not quite right. To arrive by car, rushing smoothly over the tarmac that erases all subtlety of place and height, is wrong.

Walking to Wayland's Smithy is a good haul up from the vale on to the top of the chalk ridge, the kind of rise any modern car does not notice, but sufficient, when you are walking, to place you on top of the world (Berkshire, being a county of small relief, demands not much to be got on top of). It is often breezy and – if the jumbos flying transatlantic from Heathrow are not above your head – actually quiet as few places near roads in southern England now are. The atmosphere is right; you have to, or ought to walk, since cars are banned from the Ridgeway, the old straight track by which Wayland's Smithy stands. The ancient earthwork is surrounded by beech trees, their leaves always moving, as befits an ancient sacred space.

What mood does this sacred place, and its sheltering trees offer? I have felt two responses. Both responses come from a feeling of being enclosed. While its sister-site of West Kennet sits public and open to the world on its ridge-top, with grass and ploughland around, Wayland's Smithy is hidden in a copse of trees, invisible from a distance. Because it is hidden, it feels more private, more protected from the world. That can be a good feeling; Wayland's Smithy in the embrace of sheltering beech trees. Or it can be a hostile feeling; the place is encircled, imprisoned, closed, oppressive. I do not know which response is 'authentic', and both are the responses of a twentieth-century personality.

Think of the stone circles, rings of standing stones that delimit an area. Is that central area a good place, sheltered and protected against the terrors of the world? Or is it a bad place, closing, constraining and cutting off escape into the larger world's freedoms?

It helps our mood, visiting Wayland's Smithy, to come to it by walking near other prehistoric sites and along one of the ancient green roads of England. But consider. The Ridgeway is of an unknown date, but it is not provably prehistoric. The Uffington hill-fort, by which the common path to Wayland's Smithy goes, is prehistoric but of the Iron Age, more than 3000 years more recent. The beech trees, and the little bank which also encircles (protects? shuts in?) the Smithy go back to about AD 1800, when a landowner decided to plant the barrow with firs and beeches. (The firs have gone, the beeches remain. Would we feel the same about the Smithy copse if the firs had stayed and the beeches gone?)

Wayland's Smithy has a great sense of place. But is it a sense that tells anything of prehistory?

8

Once beyond the material objects, the archaeologist walks on trembling ground, full of holes to trip and trap.

We look for motives and we find motives of a kind we find easy to comprehend. Looking back on a century now of interpretations for prehistoric Britain, one sees a most disconcerting closeness between interpretations of distant prehistory and passing contemporary concerns which they mirror faithfully. That is a hazard always; it is a particular hazard of prehistory where everything depends on interpretations of the material. For a brief period from the 1950s to the 1970s, technology was the heart of the matter – space travel! men on the moon! nuclear power too cheap to meter! computers in every home! Views of British prehistory followed obedient suit, astronomical interpretations of the monuments blossomed, and prehistoric Britain was briefly populated by the ghosts of men in white coats, not Druids this time, but 'archaeo-astronomers' documenting with precise care the slow movements in the sky of the moon's complex and irregular course. That vision, itself at some variance with the mass of evidence, has given way to a model suited to the mood of Britain in the late 1980s. Power, wealth, territorial control, the possession and display of visible riches by a successful elite – these have become the contemporary concerns which have made the new metaphors for prehistory. Evidence continues to mount for the technological accomplishments of prehistoric Britons but our interest has moved on; just as some dreams of the 1950s – space travel! computers in every home! – have arrived, they are no longer what dreams are entirely made of.

It is easy, equally, to set prehistoric people into some green and golden age; ignorant of industry, pollution and Value Added Tax they ate wholefoods, and lived in peace and harmony with each other and with their natural world. We can be sure they ate wholefoods, but the evidence is lacking for the rest of the dream. There is evidence of chronic and painful illness, of sudden death, of arrowheads in ribs and backbones, of holes cut in the bones of living skulls. The farmers came into an England that was covered in wildwood, already affected by a human presence. Within 2000 years they had converted large tracts to farmland or heath; by 500 BC, Oliver Rackham estimates, half of England had ceased to be wildwood. It was a clearance as ruthless as the one which befell the wildwoods of eastern North America in the period 1680 to

1850, and as now befalls the tropical wildwood of the Amazon basin. In the descriptions of the breaking of rural New England, one can glimpse the sorrow and the pity in the taming of the old British wilderness. See where that improving course has taken the mighty Hudson river, the grand stream of New York state, in less than three centuries. Once free-flowing, it is dammed (damned!) and canalized. The sturgeon are gone that used to go down to the sea late in autumn but come up again in spring and stay all summer, the sturgeon which the naturalist Peter Kalm saw in 1749 'all day long leaping up into the air, especially in the evening'. Where once the sturgeon swam, there lurk instead the alien carp, introduced deliberately by the US Fish Commission. Into the water itself has been poured for decades all the filth of a trash civilization: raw sewage, tannery effluents, pulp and paper wastes, long-lasting and hideously toxic PCB chemicals from electric plants. None of those – modest quantities of raw sewage apart – were dumped into the Thames by the Neolithic settlers of England, but there is nothing to show that Neolithic human nature was so very different. They simply had much less, and much less nasty junk to drop around them. I think they would have dropped their old plastic bags in the Thames, if they had plastic bags to drop.

We cannot escape from our own culture. It is hard to recognize essential concepts of our own society for the chance curiosities they are. Why, for example, is there such a thing as private ownership of land? Land is not made by human labour, nor can it be gathered up and moved about by a human being. It was there before us, and it will be there after us. Yet the idea of land ownership is deep in our culture; it is documented as running back many hundreds of years. We persuade ourselves that territoriality is a natural instinct, so universal it is present in all living animals, and we project it back on to prehistory. The distinct regional groupings of prehistory are taken as 'territories', the great monuments as expressions of that territoriality, as visible declarations of the claims to control land, and through the control of land the highroad to power and authority. Perhaps it was really so. Perhaps this image resides rather in our modern mirror, for power and authority are just what we happen to care about for ourselves.

9

I think these are the reasons why prehistory is, and ought be, an uncomfortable business. Secure knowledge is available, but that secure knowledge is material, physical, and always a little removed from what most of us feel is the heart of any history – the lives and feelings of human beings. And when we go towards those lives and feelings, we meet mirages – whether green fantasies of ecological edens, or prehistoric times peopled by yuppies in a state of perpetual self-advancement, each clutching an exotic stone-axe as the prehistoric precursor of the car-phone. And is it not better to be ignorant, and to know we are ignorant, than to delude ourselves that we know what we know not?

This where and why I find Mick Sharp's vision peculiarly fitting. It seems to me that the fairest way to see that distant past is to deal with our material knowledge of it, to address intently the evidence of flints, of pollen profiles, and of insect carapaces trapped in the Somerset peats. But at the same time, we must understand how fragmentary and narrow that material knowledge is, for it leaves out the spiritual and the irrational – those meanings and motives that in my view are likely to have been the central concerns, the real truths, of life in early British societies. The things of which we have precise knowledge are beside the point.

The Sharp pictures are magical; they make sites I know well into places that are more intense and more strange than I have seen them. They address intently the physical objects.

But they are not false, nor fantastical; no technical tricks are apparent, no air-brushed giants have been ghosted in besides the stones. Yet in their magic, in the anecdotes from stories and folklore that go with the photographs, they remind us of the gods and giants who once peopled this land, the gods and giants which a secular age has lost its faith in. That is as it should be, or at least as this archaeologist prefers it: to deal with secure knowledge and to recognize how much is lost that lies beyond reach of that knowledge.

And the photographs are precisely in the style of our age. To the places where topographic artists like Prout and Britton sketched in pencil and wash, where Edwin Smith took half-plate camera and monochrome film, there comes a photographer with a 35mm camera, patience and sensitivity – the necessities for recording the colours of artistic truth in 1989.

CHRISTOPHER CHIPPINDALE
Cambridge, summer solstice 1989

POWER

At Cairnholy I, Wigtown, burials were placed in two slab-built chambers at the eastern end of a long mound. Pits and areas of burning reveal the forecourt as the focus of rituals connected with the deposit, and periodic removal, of burial material.

The magnificent façade of whinstone slabs separated the living from the dead, and marked the changing fortunes of the sun on its journey through the day.

In early morning the stones catch the promise of the rising sun, and reflect its brilliance and power at midday. By late afternoon they cast shadows into the forecourt, where, temporarily, the powers of light and dark lie balanced. But eventually the shadows, reaching out from the chambers, banish the light as the sun slowly descends and is extinguished.

Resembling a modern sculpture park, the Stones of Stennes are the remains of a circle of 12, enclosed by the deep ditch and substantial bank of a henge, now almost levelled by ploughing.

Under the open sky, the tall, unusually shaped stones had the power to attract the attention of men and gods alike. The monument also reflects the temporal power of a ruling elite, capable of planning and executing on such a grand scale. The removal of 1250 tons (1270 tonnes) of solid sandstone from the ditch alone would have taken around 50,000 man-hours.

Until quite recently, this 'Temple of the Moon' and the nearby 'Temple of the Sun' at Brodgar (facing page, and pages 102 and 103), exercised a powerful hold over some of the local people. After praying at these places they would make marriage vows while grasping hands through a hole in the nearby Odin Stone. This stone, along with several others around Stennes, was destroyed by a local farmer, much to the dismay and anger of his neighbours.

Silbury Hill, part of the complex of remarkable Neolithic monuments around Avebury in Wiltshire, is the largest prehistoric artificial mound in Europe. 130ft (39m) high, on a base covering over 5 acres (2ha), it is a display of immense technical skill and prolongued control over labour and resources. Long believed to hold an elusive burial, it has at its core only those things characteristic of the rich and fertile landscape in which it stands – clay, flints, turf, moss, topsoil, gravel, freshwater shells, mistletoe, oak, hazel, sarsen stones, ox bones and antler tines.

Silbury is all things to all people, but its most powerful and persuasive symbolism is that of the fecund mother earth, presiding over the ceremonies of birth, life and death and the turning of the year. Similar 'harvest hills' have long been used at Lammas-tide for festivities celebrating the first fruits of the year.

Seen from near West Kennet long barrow, (page 43) Silbury Hill rises from a damp and fertile valley floor, surrounded by chalk downs bearing the light, well drained and easily worked soils so beloved by early agriculturalists.

Both views were taken on the same day. That looking over the course of the Winterbourne stream, on a balmy autumn morning. The view from West Kennet, during a hailstorm in the afternoon.

West Kennet long barrow stands open to the winds on a prominent ridge of chalk over-looking Silbury Hill.

In use for over 500 years, it housed the bones of over 40 adults and children. The skulls and long bones, charged with power, were often removed and used in ceremonies outside the tomb.

Around 3300 BC, the chambers were filled with soil and the entrance blocked by three massive stones erected across the front of the mound. Had confidence been lost in the power of the ancestors? Were they being dismissed by a new group with different customs to promote, or, had the appointed time come for their final rest, protected by mother earth and guardian spirits of stone?

The atmosphere inside Stoney Littleton long barrow, Avon, is strongly subterranean, recalling the deep caves of the Old Stone Age, used for painting and rituals of hunting magic and fertility.

Collected from outcrops over 5 miles (8km) away, these stones must have been considered particularly appropriate, and their impact, especially seen in flickering candle-light, is very strong.

(Page 47)
The stone chambers lie at the eastern end of a long mound, the horns of which create a forecourt in front of the entrance passage.

The contrast between the small stones of the revetment and the large jambs and lintel, heightens the drama of the forecourt and focuses attention on the entrance to the domain of the dead.

It is possible that corpses lay in the entrance passage, only being moved into one of the chambers when the process of decay had taken its course. This way, the newly dead could be watched and attended, and allowed to participate in the ceremonies enacted in the forecourt.

A fossil ammonite decorates the left-hand jamb with a spiral; a symbol used by many cultures to represent the passage through life and the soul's journey into death.

In a field at Avebury Trusloe, about 1 mile (1.3km) south-west of the great circle-henge of Avebury, stand Adam and Eve; the only visible remains of the Beckhampton Avenue. Adam, in the foreground, formed the eastern side of a cove; three massive stones arranged as an open box facing south-east. This cove was visually powerful, or sacred enough, to be incorporated into an avenue of around 200 sarsen stones, arranged in two parallel rows curving for 1¼ miles (2km) south-west from the circle to a point just north of the modern road. Eve, to the rear, is the sole survivor from the northern row.

These stones were known as the 'Devil's Coytes' (Quoits) and their power was taken seriously. In the years around AD 1300, the stones were systematically felled and buried in chalk-cut holes. In later centuries many of the stones at Avebury were smashed for building materials, but this careful burial suggests the neutralizing actions of zealous Christians, disturbed by the continuing pagan practises at the site.

In 1911, weighing 30 tons (30.5 tonnes), Adam fell down on his own. It took four people four weeks, to inch him back up using jacks, as he proved too powerful for traction engines and metal cables.

In the garden of the Druid's Arms – which, in the light of current thinking, should be renamed the Neolithic Astronomer Priest's Arms – at Stanton Drew in Avon, stand and lie the remains of another cove. This was a structure concerned with funerary ritual and aligned towards the moonrise at its extreme position. The Christian church was clearly troubled by the power and influence of such places, and there are many examples of churches being built in or by prehistoric sites. The most notable examples are; Knowlton in Dorset, Midmar Kirk near Aberdeen (page 121), Rudston, Humberside and Yspytty Cyfyn in Dyfed. See also Clach na h-Annait page 122.

(Page 51)
Standing 25½ft (7.8m) high, the Rudston Monolith is the tallest in Britain. Once surrounded by a henge, it formed the focus of a Neolithic ritual landscape which included four cursus monuments or processional ways. Occupying the high ground, it was a natural target for defusing by the building of a church, which, today, attracts fewer visitors than the stone.

Caught in the rich light of the dying sun, these stones at Penrhos Feilw on Anglesey, may have been the markers or guardians of a cemetery. A tradition, recorded last century, places them at the centre of a stone circle and describes the finding, between them, of a large cist containing arrowheads, spearheads and bones.

Cattle, milling around the stones of the Altarnun circle on Bodmin Moor, have worn deep hollows in the surrounding peat.

Some standing stones were erected as rubbing posts, but genuine prehistoric monuments have a power to attract animals which goes beyond the need to scratch. The stones seem to be a special place to gather, particularly in the evening. Cattle and sheep are often to be seen lying down inside stone circles or standing, apparently aimlessly, up against burial chambers and standing stones.
(Page 54)

An obliging chorus line of heifers pose beside Beersheba standing stone, Cornwall. The name is a rich source of possible practices and beliefs popularly associated with such stones.

Beer-sheba was the name Abraham gave to the place in Canaan where he settled; it is Hebrew for 'the well of an oath'.

In addition to being an intoxicating drink, beer, in the thirteenth-century, meant 'one who is', and in the seventeenth-century 'the great I am'.

Sheba = Saba; an ancient people of Yemen, and often confused with Sabaism; 'the worship of the host of heaven' – star worship.

In Cornwall, granite outcrops of distinctive shape, seem to act as magnets to the prehistoric sites which cluster around them. On the north-west of Rough Tor on Bodmin Moor, a fantastic but naturally formed arrangement was partly buried within a low, circular cairn. Showery Tor is the most striking of a number of 'burial' mounds which have at their heart, not human remains, but a stone.
(Page 56)

(Page 57)
This stone giant stands on the natural amphitheatre of Machrie Moor, Arran. (See also pages 92–93.)

Veryan round barrow is the largest in Cornwall; it comprises an outer mound of soil around a stone core.

Secondary cremations were inserted into the bottom of several narrow shafts which passed through the mound and penetrated the cairn. The primary deposit was made in a limestone cist placed on the ground surface beneath the cairn.

The barrow overlooks Gerrens Bay, across which, according to legend, Gerennius; saint and king, was rowed in a golden boat with silver oars, to be buried in the mound along with his craft.

When the cist was located and opened last century, the treasure had turned to dust and ashes.

BURIAL

With a large capstone balanced on upright slabs, Trethevy Quoit in Cornwall is a type of portal dolmen; the earliest form of burial chamber in Britain.

Their builders possessed considerable skill and judgement, arranging such heavy forms to appear light, delicately balanced and soaring.

Trethevy is surrounded by the remains of a mound which, probably, only covered the lower part of the stones and acted as a ramp to aid access to the chamber via a gap between wall and capstone.

Lurking between a sombre pool and the eerie forms of the Cheesering on Stowes Hill, Rillaton round barrow looks a natural part of Bodmin Moor.

The barrow was opened early last century when a skeleton, with a long bronze dagger and a ribbed cup of beaten gold, was found in a cist. A legend was conveniently recalled – the Cheesering was the haunt of a Druid with a magic cup. A huntsman determined to drink the cup dry but failed and, riding away in anger, was killed when his horse stumbled over the rocks.

The Bronze Age cup went missing, but was discovered in King George V's dressing room, where it served as a receptacle for the royal collar studs.

(Page 65)

The Mendip Hills around Priddy in Somerset are rich equally in lead deposits and large round barrows.

The cemetery of eight on Ashen Hill ripple across the skyline in an east–west alignment. They contain cremations in pits, urns and cists, accompanied by objects of amber, faience and bronze.

Lead was used in the production of bronze, and the families controlling this area may have grown rich on the proceeds.

Much visited, much misunderstood; Lanyon Quoit in Cornwall is a shadow of its former self. A stolid table of stone, it used to be possible to sit on horseback beneath it. The capstone lost its grip during a storm in 1815, and was re-erected only 5ft (1.5m) high in 1824.

Believed to be the burial chamber of a long mound, Lanyon Quoit is unusual in many ways and may have been more of a mausoleum or cenotaph than a grave.
(Page 66)

(Page 67)

Resembling a massive stone slug, the capstone of Lligwy burial chamber lies, balanced on three points of rubble, over a deep hole in the bedrock. This was a family vault bearing the remains of 30 individuals mixed with flints, limpet and mussel shells, and the bones of deer, dog, fowl, fox, otter, ox, pig and sheep.

Seen in autumn, the clump of beeches enclosing Wayland's Smithy forms a circle of flame against the pale surround of chalk fields. In the dappled light, the mound seems to shift and the stones of the façade change shape and size.

This is, after all, a magical place; dwelling of the lame smith of the Anglo-Saxon gods. Here the shoes for the Uffington White Horse were made, and any horse, left with a penny payment, shod by unseen hands.

In Neolithic times, the remains of 14 people were placed in a wooden mortuary house resembling a ridge tent, and covered by a small oval mound. This was later incorporated into a large wedge-shaped mound with an impressive façade, and stone chambers for more burials, at the southern end.

At Bryn Celli Ddu on Anglesey, a stone circle, accompanying cremations within a henge, was systematically destroyed before being covered by a passage grave.

What looks to be an obvious phallic symbol waits inside 'the mound in the dark grove'. But, in the chamber of a Neolithic passage grave, it is more likely to be a representation of the mother goddess, watching over the bones spread at her feet.

(Page 70)

On a wild day, at the tip of the Glenbrittle peninsula, Skye, the chamber of Rudh'an Dunain makes a welcome refuge. Now a home for foxgloves and ferns, the chamber contained the bones and cremations of Neolithic and Bronze Age people, and a foundation deposit of human and animal bones beneath one of the wall stones.

The entrance passage, rising in height towards the imposing portals of the chamber, creates a distinct psychological effect – but for whose benefit was it carefully contrived?

The isolated group of megalithic tombs in Kent's Medway Valley are situated in small pockets of pleasant countryside, hemmed in by motorways, industry and housing.

The prehistoric trade route now called the Pilgrim's Way, and the tidal River Medway, gave access to this fertile area, while sarsen stones, scattered on and around the North Downs, allowed the building of earthen long mounds with megalithic façades, chambers and kerbstones unique in eastern England.

Kit's Coty House (left), approached by an ancient trackway overhung by thorn-trees, is the remains of a burial chamber at the eastern end of a ploughed-out mound 180ft (54.9m) long. Reputedly the burial place of Catigern, a British chief killed fighting the Saxons, the site may be named after a shepherd, Christopher, who used to shelter in this 'cote' or 'cot-house'.

To the south lies Little Kit's Coty House (above), or the Countless Stones; the prone remains of a megalithic chamber and façade destroyed by a farmer in 1690.

Across the River Medway to the west, just
below the North Downs and the Pilgrim's
Way, is Coldrum long barrow, dramatically
sited on a low ridge.

The rectangular mound of earth was
retained by a kerb of sarsen stones leaning
inwards against it. The mound is now much
reduced, the kerbstones are lying flat and
those at the eastern end have slipped
downhill onto the terrace below the burial
chamber. (See also page 191)

The remains of at least 24 people, male and
female from new-born babies to adults, were
carefully arranged inside a massive stone
box bearing a great capstone and entered
by a porthole approached by paved steps.
Long-headed Neolithic people who were
short but strong. People with healthy teeth
and broad feet. People who suffered from
rheumatism later in life and had shin bones
flattened by prolongued squatting. People
who were related, and whose corpses had
been defleshed by the elements before the
broken fragments were placed in the
chamber.

One whole skeleton was found in the chamber and reburied in Meopham churchyard,
which caused the vicar of Trottiscliffe to
complain he had been robbed of his oldest
parishioner.

Reduced in height and its concentric rings of stonework revealed by excavation; the cairn on the north-west flank of Wideford Hill, Orkney, overlooks the Bay of Firth. A similar choice of site to its neighbour at Cuween, to the west.

A levelled platform was cut into the hill, and the cairn and chambers were built with great care and skill. The tiered effect may simply be a stabilising device, or have some symbolic significance – the building stages matching times of year, phases of the moon, the progressive decay of corpses, or the addition of burials. It may have been left open to view until the main chamber was filled with rubble and animal bones, and the cairn was capped with clay.
(Page 74)

One of the many legendary resting places of King Arthur, or of a rival king or giant he killed on his travels.

Arthur's Stone, Dorstone, is the remains of a Neolithic burial chamber approached by a curving entrance passage.

Dark, damp, and smelling of the earth pressing in from all sides; Hetty Peglar's Tump in Gloucestershire, retains well the atmosphere of the earth mother's womb.

The place from which were born again, through the constricted entrance, the souls of the dead, and where the bones rested securely in the belly of their creation.

Taversoe Tuick on Rousay, Orkney, is a remarkable monument having two burial chambers; one built on top of the other.
The entrance passage to the lower chamber extends southwards, beyond the cairn, as a narrowing channel ending beside a third, miniature chamber. This contained two complete pottery bowls which may have held offerings. The whole arrangement suggests a desire for communication with the contents of the lower chamber; perhaps even a form of oracle.

A platform in the lower chamber supported a crouched skeleton as if asleep on a stone bed.
The roof of the chamber forms the floor of the upper one.

(Page 80)
High in the Conwy Valley, Capel Garmon long barrow is remote, but beautifully situated looking to the hills of Snowdonia.
A triple chamber, in the centre of a trapezoidal mound, is entered by a passage from the south. The western compartment retains its capstone and was used as a stable in the 19th century.

Although the forecourt leads only to a dummy portal, it still acted as a ritual focus and was scattered with white quartz; a material of magical or religious significance. The site has been laid out to display the features described, but they were originally completely covered by a smooth mound after the tomb had been sealed.

(Page 81)
Generally, the chambered cairns on the Isle of Skye hug the coast and are sited to overlook and be seen from the sea.
Built of water-worn stones, Carn Liath – the Grey Cairn – sits beside the River Haultin only ¼ mile (0.4km) from the shore at the head of Loch Eishort; an easily recognised landmark for friend and foe alike.

The recumbent stone circle at Loanhead of Daviot near Aberdeen, was built as a monument to the moon.

A ring of ten stones ascend in height until the two tallest flank a massive recumbent slab. Within the circle lies a low mound of stone; a ring cairn, originally with an open centre. In front of the recumbent a crescentric area was kerbed off and strewn with milk white quartz. The upper surface of the recumbent was exactly horizontal and so aligned that, seen from the centre of the circle, the moon, arcing through the sky, was framed between the flankers. Around the extreme southernmost point of its 18.6-year cycle, the moon would appear to float along the levelled surface of the slab. At the centre of the circle, amidst the signs of burning, lay pits containing 5lbs (2.3kg) of human bones. Among them 50 fragments from the skulls of children – peaceful burial before a benign moon, or ritual sacrifice for a hungry god grown thin. (See also Sunhoney page 120) (Page 82)

This Bronze Age entrance grave at Bosiliack, West Penwith, has a passage which is both entrance and burial chamber.

A partial cremation with a small pot was placed inside, and a stone added to the kerb to block the entrance.

Its contents rifled, its mound worn away; the simple stone box of Chun Quoit, West Penwith, has endured. Standing on a windy ridge, it surveys heather moorland and the open sea.

(Page 85)
Seen from Arbor Low henge (page 91), on a misty November afternoon, Gib Hill round barrow was the site of a gibbet in the 18th century. In 1848, knocking away the props from his tunnel at the bottom of the mound, Thomas Bateman was suprised by the collapse of a limestone cist from just below the summit. Tumbling with the debris came a cremation and a small pottery urn.

The tumulus covered four compacted mounds of clay mixed with hazel-wood and charcoal, arranged in a square on a surface of flints and ox bones. Bateman believed the first phase of the monument was not sepulchral, and its similarity to the core of Silbury Hill (page 42) is suggestive.

After a day of heavy rain, the capstones of megalithic chambers dry in the weak sunshine of a winter afternoon.

This lonely hilltop calls to the weather; the wind was so fierce on one visit it was impossible to stand upright. On other occasions, thunder and lightning menacingly circled the hill; aiming at the trees and chambers.

The sense of isolation and the plantation of beech trees, make Minninglow Hill in Derbyshire, one of the most beautiful and poignant places I have ever been to.

SACRED AREAS

Callanish I, Isle of Lewis, Outer Hebrides.

'It is left by traditione that these were a sort
of men converted into stones by ane
Inchanter'

John Morison, 1680.

Arbor Low henge, Derbyshire. Set apart, a special place; the bank and ditch define a sacred area. (See Preface)

This setting of 4 granite boulders, circle IV, surrounded a cist containing a 'Food Vessel' urn. The elliptical stone rings, I and XI, nearby, overlay the postholes of earlier timber settings. The cremations of two men in their late twenties were placed near the centres; one in a pit, the other in an inverted urn. This ritual area has a long and complex history.
(below)

To the north-west of the complex on the moor, Auchagallon cairn watches over Machrie Bay and the outflow of the Machrie Water. (right)

(Page 92)
The peat covered moorland to the south of the Machrie Water on the Isle of Arran, is one of the most remarkable prehistoric landscapes in Britain (see also page 57). Field systems and hut circles are there for the sharp-eyed, but the remains of ceremonial sites dominate the view.
Under a storm heading for the mountains, the sandstone pillars of circle II stand sunlit. Originally of 7 or 8 stones, the ring contained two cists; one bearing an inhumation, the other a cremation.

(above)
Circle V, Fingal's Cauldron Seat, beside Moss Farm, offers a good view of the main sites on the moor below. Fingal the giant, tied his dog, Bran, to the holed stone on the outer ring, while he cooked himself a meal in the inner circle. A ruined cist was uncovered here in the last century.

(above)
The exposed burial chambers and fallen façade of Tormore cairn look north-east towards the sites on Machrie Moor.

In North Yorkshire, the area between the rivers Swale and Ure was particularly favoured; six henge monuments and numerous round barrows being built there.

The central henge at Thornborough is in a row of three running south-west by north-east, each having two opposed entrances matching this alignment, and all built to the same size and design.

Their banks were covered in crystals of gypsum, making them brilliant white in the sun and a muted glow in the mist.

Henges were places of meeting; for encounters between people and the gods of earth and sky, but they may also have served as places of guaranteed safety for such matters as trade. Stone axes were distributed widely in Neolithic Britain, often far from the source of their quarrying. Such axes have been found buried in several henges; articles of trade or religious symbols? Both, and much more.

On my last visit to Thornborough, trees, uprooted from the bank, lay scattered around and smouldering on bonfires.

Avebury; a huge circular bank, a massive ditch now only half its original depth, a great ring of 98 sarsen slabs enclosing two smaller stone circles, a cove and other settings and arrangements of stones. Walk the mile (1.6km) around the bank; gaze into the centre and wonder. The Swindon Stone, on the extreme left, guards the causeway at the northern entrance to the henge.

From Avebury's southern entrance the West Kennet Avenue runs south-east for 1½ miles (2.4km) to the Sanctuary; a complex of timber buildings and stone circles on Overton Hill.

Burials, perhaps even sacrifices, accompanied the setting up of some of the stones, and the avenue passed through an earlier ceremonial area where pits had been dug and offerings made to the earth.

The avenues are charged with symbolic possibilities, but they most probably functioned as processional ways of some sort, as folk memory at Callanish would seem to suggest (page 89). Dancing, racing, and the marching of elites in their pomp and pride have been proposed. Was an image of the god, kept in the dark of the Sanctuary, once a year uncovered, washed and then carried by priests down the avenue to its temple? Or were the avenues true sacred ways; their grass and flowers undisturbed except by the soundless passing of gods and spirits.

The Grey Cairns of Camster; two Neolithic chambered cairns in Caithness. This· site, now bleak and boggy moorland, retained its sanctity despite a dramatic change in religious ideas or cult practices.

The huge long mound engulfed two earlier round cairns containing burial chambers reached by entrance passages from the south-east. These passages were extended through the long mound, the one to the northern chamber on a different alignment revealed by a kink where the new passage meets the old entrance.

The long cairn, with its stepped profile, short horns at each end and the unusual stage-like platform fronting a shallow forecourt on the north, was surely more than a simple tomb. Something more on the lines of a cathedral raised over the grave of an early saint.

On one visit, a family in an expensive car asked me if I 'knew anything of the land hereabouts'. I never did work out if they were interested in archaeology or property speculation.

(Page 99)
Divided into three compartments by upright slabs and reached by a straight entrance passage, the southern chamber of the long cairn is very similar to that inside Camster Round.

Four stones once flanked the entrance to this Neolithic enclosure at Mayburgh, Penrith. Inside stood another setting of four stones, only one of which survives. One-and-a-half million tons of rough stones (Page 100)

form an impressively high and effective barrier to the outside world.

Unusually, Mayburgh has no internal ditch, but King Arthur's Round Table, just to the east, is a henge of the usual design.

The two circle-henges of the Ring of Brodgar and the Stones of Stennes, balanced on promontories between the lochs of Harray and Stennes on Orkney Mainland, form, along with nearby barrows, standing stones and earthworks, a remarkable ceremonial centre (see also pages 40–41).

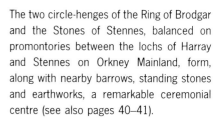

(Page 101)
Two cairns and a standing stone were placed overlooking Loch Craignish in Mid Argyll. Was this siting at Kintraw a response to the magnificence of the scenery, or a desire to involve the sun of midwinter in the life and practices of the community around

1800 BC? Looking over the site from what may be a an artificial platform on the hillslope to the north-east, the midwinter sun, after setting behind a mountain peak on Jura, would have briefly flashed into life again at the bottom of a V-shaped cleft.

The stones of Brodgar reveal a concern for geometry; sixty were erected, at equal distances, on a perfect circle of 340ft (103.7m) diameter. Exactly 125 megalithic yards – the prehistoric standard unit of length equalling 2¾ft (0.829m), proposed by Professor Thom. The size and symmetry of the site, under a limitless sky, is overwhelming (above left and page 103).

The rock-cut ditch was originally around 12ft (3.6m) deep and 30ft (9m) wide. To the south-west, the barrow of Salt Knowe rises dark from a meadow newly cut. (above)

On Bodmin Moor, three stone circles called the Hurlers run uphill in a line south-south-west by north-north-east towards the Rillaton round barrow (page 64), less than ½ mile (0.8km) away.

The stones are quite neat and regular, and a spread of quartz crystals in the central circle may have come from shaping the stones with hammers. The northern circle was crossed by a boundary bank, and two stones to the south-west could be boundary posts, although astronomical purposes have been assigned to them. Called the Pipers, legend declares them the musicians playing for a group of men turned to stone for 'profaning the Lord's Day with hurling the ball'. The Hurlers and their neighbouring barrows and enclosures stand on dismal moorland amidst the scars and ruins of the tin mining industry.

Causewayed camps; large enclosures formed by deep discontinuous ditches surrounding steep-sided banks pierced by entrances, were built early in the Neolithic, and were the first expressions of communal effort on a large scale.

The 4 acre (1.4ha) site at Knap Hill, Wiltshire, is smaller than average; it may not have been completed and finds from the site are few. Remains at similar sites include houses, animal bones, domestic refuse, and pots, tools and even stones from far outside the local area. At a few sites, human skulls, bones and whole skeletons were arranged at the bottom of freshly cut ditches.

The camps were most probably meeting-places, occupied seasonally by people from a wide area, for a mixture of secular and ritual activities. Autumn fairs where cattle were slaughtered, goods traded, bargains made and marriages arranged; all with a background of feasting and ceremony.

Some sites, such as Windmill Hill near Avebury, had mortuary areas where corpses were exposed before burial on site, or in a nearby tomb. Human sacrifice, cannibalism and infanticide have all been hinted at.

Many of the camps are dramatically sited. Here, looking eastwards, Knap Hill clings to the southern edge of the Marlborough Downs overlooking the Vale of Pewsey. Just to the west, the contemporary long barrow of Adam's Grave, occupies a similar position.

Prehistoric people knew their environment; the fertile soils, the sheltered spots, the best rock outcrops, and where seams of flint lay buried. They understood the strategic value of certain locations and how to place their monuments for maximum visibility and impact. They were also sensitive to the spirit of place and responded to the strangeness and visual power of certain landscapes. Carn Ban cairn on Skye, stands above Staffin Bay and echoes the volcanic piles of Dun Mor and Dun Beag dumped before the haunting Quiraing ridge.
(Page 108)

(Page 109)
The standing stones on the north shore of Loch Eyre on Skye, seem to complete the scene. Carn Liath cairn (page 81), is just over ½ mile (1 km) to the south-east, and another cairn a little less to the north-west.
Local folklore names them Sornaichean nam Feinne; the Stones of the Giants, which, with a third stone, supported a cooking pot large enough to stew a whole deer. While trying to take this photograph, a party of trippers marched in front of the camera and tripod and scattered the sheep – it took a long time to coax the sheep back into place. A little later at the stones, I met Robbie the Pict and discussed the Pictish Free State, symbol stones and philosophy – an eventful day.

The Rollright Stones, Oxfordshire; 77 lumps of weathered limestone, the bewildering remains of around 20 uprights laid out in an exact circle. Folk customs and tales about the site reverberate with the possibilities of prehistoric ceremony. At midnight on New Year's Day, the stones processed downhill to drink at a spring. Young people would meet at the stones 'at a special time and make merry with cakes and ale'. In plea for a child, barren wives would visit the circle at midnight and press their naked breasts against the stones. Rumours and sightings of witches using the circle at night, persisted until very recently.
The Whispering Knights; the remains of a burial chamber, and the King Stone monolith (pages 17, 155), complete this unusual and atmospheric complex.

For at least 400 years during the Bronze Age, the Fechan Valley in Clwyd, now partly covered by the Llyn Brenig reservoir, was used as a place of ceremony and burial. Some of the monuments have been reconstructed and form an archaeological trail on the eastern side of the lake.

(above)
Brenig 46, a simple round cairn containing cremations.
(above right)
Brenig 44, a ring cairn surrounded by a circle of wooden posts; the posts may have been taller and painted, carved or decorated in some way. To begin with, only charcoal was buried in pits within the ring, but around 140 years later human cremations began to be placed in the central area. To the rear is Brenig 45, Boncyn Arian – Money Hillock. A plain barrow covered a complex series of stake-holes and a drystone wall encircling a central grave. Later cremations were inserted into the mound including the burnt ear-bones of an infant placed in an urn. The similar use of such bones has been recorded at other sites.

(Page 113)
Brenig 51, a platform cairn reconstructed with its centre open; at a later stage the centre was filled in to form a completely smooth platform. Cremated bones were placed in the central area and under various parts of the cairn. At the very centre, commanding this unearthly stage, stood a large post; a carved totem or may-pole.

Stone rows. What are they? Processional ways, astronomical alignments, pointers to topographically significant features, boundary markers, signposts on prehistoric routes, spirit channels for the dead, one of the responses of prehistoric dowsers to the movement of underground water – the list goes on.

The Nine Maidens stone row on St Breock Down, Cornwall. On a bleak winter's day, a long cold wait standing in a wet ditch, was rewarded by a flicker of sun.

The eastern end of this double stone row at Merrivale on Dartmoor, is blocked by a large triangular stone. It has a cairn at its centre and, along with another double row just to the north, is part of a complex including a stone circle, standing stones, a burial cist and numerous hut circles – the houses of the Bronze Age people who created and used this sacred area.

Clustered near the coast at the head of Loch Roag on Lewis in the Outer Hebrides, are at least ten groups of standing stones; all variations on a theme. On a promontory to their west and dominating the view is Callanish I; their focus and inspiration.

An avenue from the north-north-east approaches a circle surrounding a tall pillar and a passage grave. Three rows of stone approach, approximately, from the remaining cardinal points. Like the stubborn mist, legend and folklore cling to the stones. In the 18th century, local people were still drawn to them, especially on midsummer morning when the 'Shining One' walked along the avenue heralded by the cuckoo's song. Forbidden by the Ministers, the people continued in secret 'for it would not do to neglect the stones'.
(Page 116)

(Page 117)
On a hill to the south-south-east of Callanish I, is Garynahine or Ceann Hulavig, Callanish IV. A low central stone enclosed in a cairn and surrounded by an oval setting of five uprights.

At Loch Roag or Cnoc Ceann a'Gharaidh, Callanish II, two fallen stones and five uprights form an ellipse around a ruined cairn. In October, the sun, when viewed from beside the monolith in the main circle, is seen to rise directly behind Callanish II. Many such alignments may be accidental, but the builders of this complex do seem to have been aware and interested in the movements of the sun and moon.
(upper left)

(lower left)
Standing amidst peat cuttings, on a low ridge to the east-south-east of the main circle, is Cnoc Fillibhir Bheag, Callanish III. Two concentric ellipses with eight stones remaining on the outer ring, four on the inner and several more fallen and buried.

(Page 119)
The smooth silvery stones of Lewisian gneiss have a light of their own and appear luminous in all weathers.
The building of Callanish I was never fully completed and the passage grave, just visible amongst the uprights, was an unusual late addition. A conscious act of archaism or, as at Bryn Celli Ddu (page 72), the desecration of a rival.

At Sunhoney recumbent stone circle, Grampian, the rooks call in a ring of trees, which surrounds the circle as the stones surround a ring cairn, at the centre of which was found cremated bone and the remains of a pyre. (See also Loanhead of Daviot, page 82).

The recumbent stone bears 31 cup-marks which, at this type of site, seem to indicate and symbolize certain positions of the moon. It faces the south-west, and is seen here in a tangle of light and shade from the falling sun. At other times the moon will first break free of the hills and, seen from the centre of the circle, appear to rise above the recumbent, its arc caught between the flanking stones for an hour or so.

Sunhoney may have been a sombre shrine to the moon; eerie in the pale light of its god. It may still, as rumour has it, be the haunt of black magicians, but on one May evening, in the sensible company of the dogs from the farm, it seemed a wholesome place.

(Page 121)
At the nearby Midmar Kirk, a graveyard was laid out around the recumbent stone circle in 1914. The circle was landscaped and the ring cairn replaced by a neat circle of grass. A clash of cultures, religious ideas and aesthetic judgement. A pale shadow of a cross lingers on the grass while the circle waits for the moon.

Early saints and missionaries to the Hebrides were urged to build churches wherever they found standing stones. A stone and well at Kilbride on the Isle of Skye, 'associated with heathen worship', attracted the attention of St Maelrubba and his followers from Iona, who built a church, dedicated to St Bridgit, nearby. They blessed the well and stone calling them Tobar na h-Annait and Clach na h-Annait – the Well (and stone) of the Mother Church.

Until the last century, it was firmly believed that in the now holy well 'a little fish had lived from age to age, preserved alive by some mysterious power'. Photographed on a 'soft day' in June, Clach na h-Annait stands at the foot of Beinn Dearg Bheag, with the well hidden amidst the flags in marshy ground below.

(Page 123)
Cnocan nan Gobhar long cairn – Goat's Knowe – at Kilmarie on the Isle of Skye. Clothed in lush vegetation, luminous green under the trees, it is easy to see why such cairns were considered to be fairy mounds harbouring fabulous beasts.

Maes Howe chambered cairn on Orkney, was built on an artificially levelled platform and encircled by a low ring of stone and turves. This was added to in the 10th century AD when the tomb may have been reused for a Norse burial. The bank has been enlarged again in modern times. It formed a symbolic barrier around a sacred area which, itself, lies within one of the most dramatic ceremonial landscapes in Britain.

SYMBOLS AND IMAGES

A cup with a double ring and a horned spiral
at Achnabreck, Argyll.

Barclodiad y Gawres — the Apronful of the Giantess — is one of only two examples on Anglesey of an Irish form of passage grave (see also Bryn Celli Ddu, page 11). The tomb's interior is decorated with a style of megalithic art rare in Britain, but very common in Brittany and Ireland. Wavy lines, zigzags, spirals, lozenges and chevrons adorn five of the stones; three of which guard the entrance to the chamber at the inner end of the passage.

The individual images may symbolize concepts, the powers and attributes of gods or spirits, or the energy of natural forces such as wavy lines for water. But, when combined and used as on the tall upright opposite, the suggestion of a stylized and absract rendering of a figure is very strong. As in Britanny, this may be the mother goddess; the tomb being simultaneously her home and representation, with the swollen chambers and narrow entrance symbolic of the struggle to be born.

A sloping slab at Roughting Linn in Northumberland has been covered with over sixty cup-and-ring marks – deliberately formed hollows surrounded by circular grooves. Some of these, with a line leading to the centre, bear a superficial resemblance to maze patterns named after the city of Troy, where horsemen would weave intricate patterns at funeral games. They symbolize the inner secrets of life and death, and the patterns can be followed in dance to represent such things as death and rebirth.

An Iron Age fort lies just to the west of the carvings with the waterfall or 'linn' beyond it. (Page 130)

Carvings and another Iron Age fort lie close together on Dod Law near Wooler. This led to the idea that the carvings were plans of local forts and settlements, but there is no proven correspondence, and the carvings are now believed to be from the Bronze Age. However, recent research in the Alps has found a link between marks on carved rocks and the siting of contemporary settlements, with the cups and wandering channels marking springs and water courses.

Some dowsers in Britain claim that prehistoric ceremonial sites were positioned and laid out in response to the presence and movement of underground water. The diagrams they draw showing meandering lines linking points and spirals of blind springs etc, do bear a remarkable resemblance to some of the rock carvings.

To grind hollows in stone seems to be an ancient, deep-rooted and widespread human habit. Cup-marks are found in all the countries of Europe, the whole of Africa, America, Russia and Australia; the earliest reliably dated examples being made by Neanderthal people over 100,000 years ago. Obviously, the same image does not necessarily always symbolize the same idea, but there is a recurring association between cup-marks and death and funerary ritual.

At Bachwen, Gwynedd, the upper surface of the capstone of a Neolithic burial chamber is decorated with 110 cup-marks.

(Page 133)
Pecked carvings decorate the lintel of a cell entrance inside Holm of Papa Westray South chambered cairn, Orkney. The 'eye-brow' motifs have Continental and Aegean affinities. They are also similar to the owlish eyes and eyebrows carved, with geometric figures, on small drums of chalk deposited with the burial of a five-year-old child inside a barrow at Folkton, North Yorkshire.

This impressive slab at High Banks, Galloway, has a central cup-mark with widely spaced rings surrounded by a mass of simple cups. Such stones were once seen as Druidic altars designed to catch the blood flowing from sacrificial victims. The carvings at some sites will hold liquids, but many others are on vertical faces or at steep angles on sloping surfaces.

In various parts of Scotland, particularly Argyll and the Isles, rainwater was collected from the cups for its healing powers and fertile properties.

To ensure a good supply of milk and the continued goodwill of the 'wee folk' – the fairies – offerings, usually of milk, were placed in the hollows of carved stones.

A kerbstone retaining the cairn of the north-east passage grave at Balnuaran of Clava near Inverness, is studded with cup-marks, along with meandering grooves and a cup-and-ring. The Clava cairns are surrounded by stone circles and are similar to the recumbent stone circles of Grampian in their south-west orientation, and the use of cup-marks and quartz (see pages 82 and 120). The presence of cup-marks at such a site strengthens their association with death, the midwinter setting sun and different positions of the moon.

Five cairns stand in a north–south row – a linear cemetery – in the Kilmartin Valley, Argyll. They demonstrate the progression from communal burial in chambered cairns in the Neolithic, to individual burials in cists inside solid cairns, in the Bronze Age.

A burial cist and capstone may be viewed in a modern chamber inside Nether Largie North round cairn. The slab, covered with around 40 cup-marks overlain by 10 axeheads, was placed face down with the symbols staring into the darkness of the cist. Two more axeheads face into the cist from the end-slab. They are flat bronze axes of a type traded from Ireland in the early Bronze Age. In the Neolithic, stone axes were buried, unused or deliberately smashed, in ceremonial monuments. Their size, workmanship and quality of materials, and the circumstances of their burial show they were far more than functional objects. Bronze axes also had status and power, but as the nature of society and religious beliefs as indicated by burial practices, had dramatically changed, so too may the meaning of the axe.

To some cultures, axes were symbols of the sun and, along with the hammer, the symbol and weapon of the god of war. Stone axes were the gift of mother earth, lovingly shaped by her people. Bronze axes were her gifts transformed by the magical powers of men. Born and shaped in fire, they reflected the colour and light of the sun.

At Baluachraig in the Kilmartin Valley, Argyll, over 130 cups and 23 cup-and-rings lie on a smooth outcrop of gritstone sloping southwards.

In southern Scotland, many, but not all, carved outcrops are near a source of copper or gold. This has led to speculation that the cup-and-ring carvings were used in religio-magical ceremonies by metal prospectors who may have formed guilds or brotherhoods linked by secret rites.

Some of the carvings could have been used as lamps to burn oil or wax, and it is possible to envisage ceremonies, on a still night, enacted before an outcrop ablaze with flickering lights.

Rombolds Moor, to the south of Ilkley in West Yorkshire, was an area of intense prehistoric activity and is littered with carved rocks and outcrops. This unique design on the millstone grit of the Hanging Stones, occupies a commanding position on the north-east edge of the moor.

Sheets of mist and rain mask the view over Ilkley and to the Wharfe Valley beyond.

The surface of this cup-and-ring marked boulder at Newbiggin, Perth, seems alive with rippling forms reminiscent of the movement of a painted or tattooed body.

(Page 142)
Tŷ-mawr standing stone, Anglesey. Evocatively shaped standing stones have long been seen as the stylized representations of divine or human forms, and folklore tells of many unfortunate people turned to stone. Upright pillars and triangular or lozenge shapes suggest the male and female sexual organs, reinforcing the long association of the stones with fertility.

(Page 143)
Men Gurta – the Stone of Waiting – on St Breock Down, Cornwall, looks very much like a bolt from the sky-god sent to fertilize the earth. Standing in a cairn of quartz, its dark gritstone white-veined with quartz; the material used in so many prehistoric rituals, it must have appeared particularly potent.

One of the most spectacularly decorated outcrops in Britain lies at Ormaig, Argyll, where 'ring rosettes' jostle with more common symbols on a slab of schist in view of Loch Craignish.

Visits were made to this remote site in a variety of weather conditions, and at different times of the day, but it was the low sunshine of late evening which produced the most graphic effect.

(Page 145)
An impressive rock below Lordenshaws hillfort in Northumberland, bears cups, rings, basins and channels. The clarity of the carvings was improved by spraying them with water; a less damaging and misleading technique than chalking them in.

Well into Christian times, pebbles were placed in hollows and stone basins, and turned for good luck or as a curse.

A 'spider's web' pattern at Achnabreck, Argyll, comprising a central cup with seven rings cut by radial grooves.

Possible explanations for Neolithic and Bronze Age art motifs are endless.

Obviously, they meant something specific and important to the people who spent so much time in their creation, and they were far more than mere decoration.

Whatever their meaning, I believe many were based on natural forms – currents in water, air and smoke, growth patterns in wood, shell, bone and plants, the development of a foetus and the spirally arranged internal organs of a cow. These outward manifestations of creative forces would have been very familiar to prehistoric people and easily expressed in abstract form.

(Page 148)
As raindrops falling on a still pool, cups-and-rings shimmer on the surface of the rock at Cairnbaan, near Lochgilphead, Argyll.

(Page 149)
At Kilmichael Glassary in Argyll, keyhole designs and unusually large cup-marks cover the outcrop, and one carving is suspiciously foot-sized and shaped. Similarly shaped stones were used in the early medieval period, during the inauguration ceremonies of the Irish kings of this area. And in Tunisia, on rocks bearing ancient cup-marks, newly-weds still chisel around their feet as oath and marriage document.

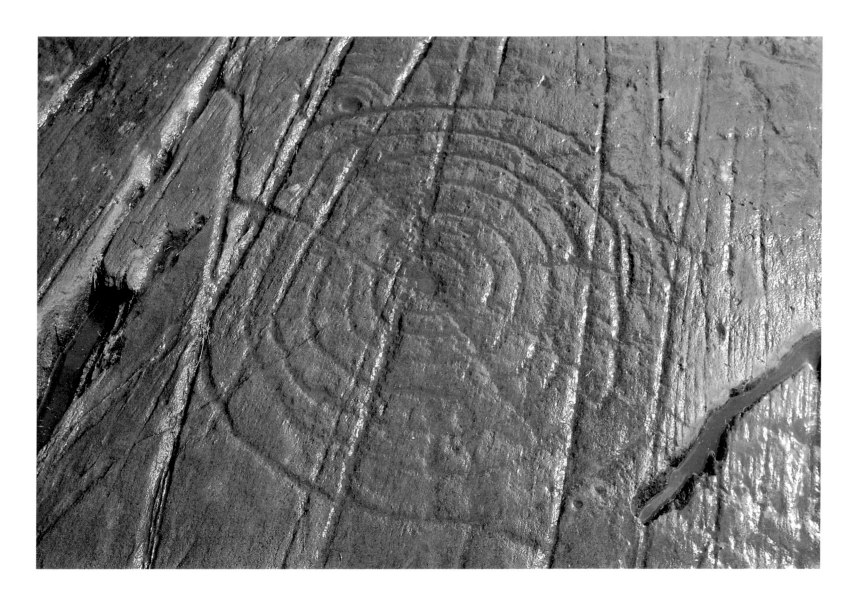

Chambered cairns were probably as elaborate in their use and symbolism as a medieval cathedral. Incorporating the cross, and, in numbers and images, references to the Gospels, Christian architecture contains, in symbolic form, the substance of the idea which inspired it.

Native peoples in different countries lay out the ground plans of their houses in imitation of their fertile goddess. Some North American Indians used to expose corpses in mortuary houses modelled on domestic dwellings. Similar processes can be glimpsed in the British Neolithic, with chambered cairns being a mixture of 'cathedral', body of the goddess and houses of the dead.

At Maes Howe on Orkney (page 125), the passage and blocking stone were so arranged as to allow the midwinter setting sun to briefly illuminate the chamber wall. People who put so much skill and effort into stage-managing such effects, knew well the power of symbols.

Unstan chambered cairn, Orkney Mainland.

(Page 150)
Zennor Quoit, West Penwith, Cornwall.

No-one knows for certain what the Men-an-Tol, in West Penwith, is. The present arrangement of three stones is quite recent, but the central stone looks like the porthole entrance to a Neolithic tomb, which may explain some of the folk customs at the site. Also known as the Crickstone, children were passed through the hole to cure rickets and skin diseases, and adults could banish their ague by crawling through 'nine times against the sun'.

Two brass pins placed crosswise on the stone would, by their movement, answer questions.

Bones, a kind of rebirth from illness and an oracle – it all sounds very familiar.

ANCIENT STONES IN CHANGING LANDSCAPES

A would-be king turned to stone by a witch, and a focus, into modern times, of activities connected with feasting and fertility. The King Stone in Oxfordshire, was the marker-stone for an early Bronze Age cemetery of small cairns.

Stranded by ploughing or engulfed by crops, Duddo Four Stones circle (there are five stones), clings to a knoll in the Till Valley, Northumberland. Labourers turned into blocks of sandstone for picking turnips on the Sabbath, it seems fitting they should be such close witnesses to the agricultural process.

Maen y Bardd dolmen stands high on the slopes overlooking the Conwy Valley, in an area rich in prehistoric remains. Burial cairns, a stone circle, standing stones, a fort, settlements and field systems are strung out along the course of a prehistoric route from the north coast, through a mountain pass, into the Conwy Valley. The Romans followed this route and built a fort at Caerhun, near a ford on the River Conwy. A part of the same route was used by the electricity board for their plyons, and by an oil company for a pipeline. Ramblers now pass many of these ancient sites by, unnoticed, on their way to or from the Youth Hostel at Rhiw.

Rhiw standing stone. A once thriving landscape is now rough pasture covered in bracken and thistles. Home of hardy sheep and Welsh mountain ponies who graze where they can, and follow the rich green strips where springs come to the surface.

Unmistakebly alien in a well ordered landscape of arable farming, Duggleby Howe is a Neolithic round barrow within a ploughed-out henge. A rare survivor of the intensive agriculture which has destroyed so many of the upstanding remains of prehistory on the Yorkshire Wolds.

On scruffy land immediately east of the A841 Brodick to Lamlash road on Arran, six stones, graded in height, form a circle around a burial cist. Passed largely unseen by people in rushing cars, the circle is losing its wide views as the dreary forestry plantations inch higher.

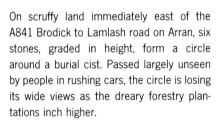

Its mound spread by repeated ploughing, a few stones of the south-east chamber are all that remain of the Devil's Den chambered long mound near Avebury in Wiltshire.

In the early 18th century, the capstone lay horizontally on vertical supports, and there were at least five more stones in the arrangement.

The Devil is blamed for most of the damage, as he visits the site at midnight and tries to move the capstone.

Underpinning and bedding-in the chamber in concrete in 1921, seems to have put a stop to the Devil's destruction of his den, but it has not saved the mound from the plough.

(Page 164)
At Stanton Drew in Avon, the remains of three stone circles, two avenues and a cove (see page 50), form a complex south of the River Chew. Known as 'The Weddings', they are a party, including the parson, turned to stone for continuing their festivities through Saturday night into Sunday morning.

Missing the companionship of its fellows, one of the remaining avenue stones looks toward an upstart tree.

On a narrow shelf of moorland between the Loch of Housetter and the steep granite screes of the Beorgs of Housetter, stand the mutilated remains of two chambered cairns. A third, smaller and better preserved, stands high up the slope amongst the scree.

The stones have been robbed over the years for road metal and an intrusive strip of modern tarmac now runs along this spectacular piece of land.

The southern tomb, with its striking red granite standing stones and grey cairn, is known locally as the 'Giant's Grave.'
(Page 165)

Exquisitely sculptural, the stones on Lundin Links, Fife, rear before a sea of yellow rape. Erected to observe the minimum moonrise and moonset, dug under in the 18th century when 'bones of men' were found in coffins, they now stand on the second fairway of the Ladies Golf Club.

Photographing from the safety of the rough, it was fascinating to watch the balls, hit straight and true, fly gracefully between the stones.

Around 1800 BC, it would have been possible, using the stones at Ballochroy, Kintyre, and the right-hand slope of Corra Beinn on Jura to the north-west, to establish whether or not the summer solstice had past.

The setting position of the sun has changed over the years, robbing the stones of their precision, but the sunset over the Paps of Jura is still a beautiful sight.

Trying to photograph this, I was annoyed to find a submarine positioned between stone and peak. I returned the following evening – the submarine was still there.

Llech Idris, near Trawsfynydd, Gwynedd, was erected near a prehistoric route associated with metal prospecting and trading in the Bronze Age. Whether route-marker or memorial, it was placed to be seen in an upland landscape more densely populated than now.

One winter day, the only occupants of this remote landscape were a cold photographer and his companion, and a farmer feeding his sheep. Seeing the camera equipment, and worried we might be digging around the stone, he and his dogs came to check us out, and stayed to tell us stories.

He told us the legend of the giant Idris Gawr hurling the stone 10 miles (16km) from the summit of Cader Idris; that the metal-bearing rocks in the valley attract thunder storms, and how a girl, carrying a basket of iron shears down from the hills behind the stone, was struck by lightning and killed.

The four concentric circles with a central barrow at Yellowmead is unique on Dartmoor. Packed with prehistoric cairns, cists, standing stones, circles, rows, hut circles and field systems; Dartmoor was home for many people in the Bronze Age, before lower temperatures, increased rainfall and accelerated peat growth made such upland areas inhospitable.
(Page 170)

(Page 171)
On sombre moorland at Unival, North Uist, stand the remains of a Neolithic chambered cairn where, in the Iron Age, people built a round house and used the burial chamber as a cooking pit.
Now, the area is covered in thick, dark, wet, ankle-turning peat; cut by the local people for their sweet smelling fires.
The trudge across the moor to this desolate place, was enlivened by the sight of red deer on a ridge; dark forms against the mist and rain.

The stones at Trellech in Gwent, are said to be the result of long distance hurling by the wizard Jack o'Kent, or the memorial of a great battle fought by King Harold of England.
Three pillars of conglomerate or 'pudding stone', gently lean, ever nearer the grass of quiet pasture, in sight of farm and church.

The Giant's Stones, Hamnavoe, Shetland, look a natural part of the moorland which has grown around them.
Originally a row of three aligned east–west, they point to, and are visible from, the bay below.

Three burial cairns were built on a hilltop in view of the distinctive outcrops of Carn Meini in the Preseli Hills, Dyfed.

This special dolerite; blue-grey with large white spots, was used to make stone axes, and for the short-lived 'bluestone' circle at Stonehenge, 135 miles (217km) away.

These strange outcrops still draw the eye and dominate the surrounding landscape, but we do not feel the urge to transport them to Wiltshire.

The people of Neolithic and Bronze Age Britain had responses to the natural world and compulsions very different from our own. But, while not understanding their motives, we can still appreciate their ability to place monuments in the landscape so they feel just right.

They manipulated their environment in a way that still satisfied the spirit, in sharp contrast to many present-day efforts, which simply deaden and depress.

GAZETEER

When the Long Stone, at Minchinhampton in Gloucestershire, hears the clock strike midnight, it runs around the field.

This book is not a guide to the sites but the following few comments and gazeteer may be helpful.

The gazeteer gives the name, type and location of a site and the page on which a photograph appears. This is followed by the sheet of the Ordnance Survey 1:50,000 Landranger Map series; the most useful for the tourist and general visitor. For those with the old 1″ maps, the number is given in brackets ( ). The National Grid reference is given to 6 figures. Finally, whether the site is in the care of the following bodies is noted: Cadw – Welsh Historic Monuments (C), English Heritage – Historic Buildings and Monuments Commission (EH), Historic Buildings and Monuments – Scottish Development Department (HBM-SDD), The National Trust (NT).
All these organisations have membership schemes and publish newsletters, magazines and guides to their properties. Unless otherwise stated there is free access at any reasonable time to the sites in their care included in this book.

All the other sites are on private land of some sort. For those on or near public footpaths access is usually permitted by custom, but if there is any doubt, permission should be sought at the nearest house or farm. Ancient monuments and their would-be visitors can be a headache for landowners, so please ask permission, be courteous, follow the country code and, especially, keep children and dogs under control.

ACHNABRECK cup-and-ring marks, Lochgilphead, Argyll (pages 17, 127, 147). OS Map 55 (52), NR 856907 (HBM-SDD).

ADAM and EVE standing stones (remains of Beckhampton Avenue), Beckhampton, Avebury, Wiltshire (page 49). OS Map 173 (157), SU 089693.

ALTARNUN NINE STONES stone circle, Bodmin Moor, Cornwall (page 54). OS Map 201 (186), SX 236782.

ARBOR LOW henge and stone circle, Middleton, Youlgrave, Derbyshire (page 91). OS Map 119 (111), SK 160636 (EH). The farmer owns the right of way and makes a charge for its use. Gib Hill round barrow is just to the south-west.

ARTHUR'S STONE megalithic tomb, Dorstone, Bredwardine, Hereford and Worcester (page 75). OS Map 148 (142), SO 319431 (EH).

ASHEN HILL round barrow group, Priddy, Somerset (page 65). OS Map 182 (165), ST 539515.

AUCHAGALLON cairn/stone circle, Machrie Bay, Arran (page 93). OS Map 69 (66), NR 893346 (HBM-SDD).

AVEBURY henge and stone circles, nr. Marlborough, Wiltshire (page 96). OS Map 173 (157), SU 103700 (EH, NT).

BACHWEN dolmen, Clynnogfawr, Gwynedd (page 132). OS Map 115 (115), SH 407495.

BALLOCHROY standing stones and cist, Kintyre, Argyll (page 167). OS Map 62 (58), NR 730525.

BALLYMEANOCH standing stones (and henge), Kilmartin Valley, Argyll (page 9). OS Map 55 (52), NR 833965.

BALUACHRAIG cup-and-ring marks, Kilmartin Valley, Argyll (page 138). OS Map 55 (52), NR 832969 (HBM-SDD).

BARCLODIAD-Y-GAWRES burial chamber (passage grave), Rhosneiger, Anglesey, Gwynedd (page 129). OS Map 114 (106), SH 328708 (C). Key available from 'Wayside Cafe', Llanfaelog.

BEERSHEBA standing stone, Trevarrack, St Ives, Cornwall (page 55). OS Map 203 (189), SW 525372.

BEORGS OF HOUSETTER, The Giant's Grave standing stones and cairn, North Roe, Shetland (page 165). OS Map 3 (2), HU 361854.

BOSILIACK cairn (entrance grave), Ding Dong Mine, nr. Morvah, West Penwith, Cornwall (page 83). OS Map 203 (189), SW 431342.

BRENIG Bronze Age cemetery, nr. Cerrig-y-Drudion, Clwyd (pages 112, 113). OS Map 116 (108), SH 983574 and area. (Welsh Water Authority.) Visitor's centre and archaeological trails beside Llyn Brenig reservoir.

BRYN CELLI DDU burial chamber (passage grave and henge), Llandaniel Fab, Anglesey, Gwynedd (pages 13, 61, 70). OS Map 114 (106), SH 508702 (C). Sometimes locked – key available at farm.

CAIRNBAAN cup-and-ring marks, Lochgilphead, Argyll (page 148). OS Map 55 (52), NR 838911 (HBM-SDD).

CAIRNHOLY chambered cairns, nr. Creetown, Wigtown District, Dumfries and Galloway (page 39). OS Map 83 (73+80), NX 517538 (HBM-SDD). Cairnholy II at NX 518540.

CALLANISH I passage grave, monolith, stone circle, and avenues, Isle of Lewis, Outer Hebrides (pages 15, 89, 116, 119). OS Map 13 (12), NB 213331 (HBM-SDD).

CALLANISH II stone circle, Cnoc Ceann a'Gharaidh, Loch Roag, Isle of Lewis, Outer Hebrides (page 118). OS Map 13 (12), NB 222326.

CALLANISH III stone circle, Cnoc Fillibhir Bheag, Isle of Lewis, Outer Hebrides (page 118). OS Map 13 (12), NB 225326.

CALLANISH IV stone circle and cairn, Ceann Hulavaig, Garynahine, Isle of Lewis, Outer Hebrides (page 117). OS Map 13 (12), NB 230304.

CAMSTER LONG chambered horned cairn, Watten, Lybster, Caithness (pages 98, 99). OS Map 12 (16), ND 260442 (HBM-SDD). Access to interior via low, narrow passages, but worth the effort. Lit by rooflights so no need for a torch.

CAMSTER ROUND chambered cairn, Watten, Lybster, Caithness (page 98). OS Map 12 (16), ND 261440 (HBM-SDD). Rooflights, no need for torch.

CAPEL GARMON chambered long mound, nr. Betws-y-Coed, Gwynedd (page 80). OS Map 116 (107), SH 818544 (C).

CARN BAN cairn, Staffin Bay, Trotternish, Isle of Skye (page 108). OS Map 23 (24), NG 487683.

CARN LIATH chambered cairn, Kensaleyre, Trotternish, Isle of Skye (page 81). OS Map 23 (24), NG 420514.

CARN MEINI dolerite outcrop (source of Stonehenge bluestones), Preseli Hills, Dyfed (page 175). OS Map 146 (139), SN 140320.

CHUN QUOIT, Morvah, West Penwith, Cornwall (page 84). OS Map 203 (189), SW 403339.

CLACH NA H-ANNAIT standing stone, Kilbride, Torrin, Isle of Skye (page 122). OS Map 32 (25), NG 590203.

CLAVA chambered cairns and stone circles, Inverness, Highland (page 135). OS Map 27 (28), NH 757444 (HBM-SDD).

CNOCAN NAN GOBHAR long cairn, Kilmarie, Strathaird, Isle of Syke (page 123), OS Map 32 (34), NG 553174.

COLDRUM chambered long barrow, Trottiscliffe, Maidstone, Kent (pages 73, 191). OS Map 188 (171), TW 654607 (NT).

DEVIL'S DEN burial chamber, Clatford Bottom, Avebury, Wiltshire (page 163). OS Map 173 (157), SU 152697.

DOD LAW rock carvings, Doddington Moor, Wooler, Northumberland (page 131). OS Map 75 (64), NU 005317.

DUDDO FOUR STONES stone circle, Till Valley, Northumberland (page 157). OS Map 75 (64), NT 931437.

DUGGLEBY HOWE round barrow, Duggleby, North Yorkshire (page 160). OS Map 101 (92), SE 881669.

FOEL TRIGARN cairn (SW of 3), Preseli Hills, Dyfed (page 175). OS Map 146 (139), SN 158336. Carn Meini dolerite outcrop, source of Stonehenge bluestones, to rear.

GIANT'S STONES standing stones, Hamnavoe, Eshaness, Shetland (page 173). OS Map 3 (2), HU 243806.

GIB HILL round barrow, Middleton, Youlgrave, Derbyshire (page 85). OS Map 119 (111), SK 161636 (EH). Just SW of Arbor Low henge and stone circle.

HANGING STONES rock carvings, Ilkley Moor, West Yorkshire (page 139). OS Map 104 (96), SE 128467.

HAROLD'S STONES standing stones, Trellech, Monmouth, Gwent (page 172). OS Map 162 (155), SO 496052.

HETTY PEGLER'S TUMP chambered long barrow, Uley, Gloucestershire (page 77). OS Map 162 (156), SO 790001. If locked, key available at farm downhill on right. Torch needed.

HIGH BANKS cup-and-ring marks, Kirkcudbright, Stewarty, Dumfries and Galloway (page 134). OS Map 84 (81), NX 709489.

HOLM OF PAPA WESTRAY SOUTH chambered cairn, Papa Westray, Orkney (page 133). OS map 5 (5), HY 509518 (HBM-SDD).

HURLERS stone circles, Minions, Bodmin Moor, Cornwall (page 105). OS Map 201 (186), SX 258714 (EH).

KILMICHAEL GLASSARY cup-and-ring marks, Kilmartin Valley, Argyll (page 149). OS Map 55 (52), NR 858935 (HBM-SDD).

KING STONE standing stone, Rollright, Oxfordshire (pages 19, 155). OS Map 151 (145), SP 206309. Just across the road from the Rollright Stones stone circle.

KINTRAW cairns and standing stone, Loch Craignish, Argyll (page 101). OS Map 55 (52), NM 830050.

KIT'S COTY HOUSE burial chamber, Aylesford, Maidstone, Kent (page 72). OS Map 188 (172), TQ 745608 (EH).

KNAP HILL causewayed camp, Alton Barnes, Devizes, Wiltshire (pages 106, 107). OS Map 184 (167), SU 121636.

LAMLASH stone circle, beside A841 Brodick to Lamlash road, Arran (page 161). OS Map 69 (66), NS 018336.

LANYON QUOIT, Morvah, West Penwith, Cornwall (page 66). OS Map 203 (189), SW 430337 (NT).

LITTLE KIT'S COTY HOUSE, THE COUNTLESS STONES Aylesford, Maidstone, Kent (page 72). OS Map 188 (172), TQ 745604 (EH).

LLECH IDRIS standing stone, Trawsfynydd, Gwynedd (page 169). OS Map 124 (116), SH 731311.

LLIGWY burial chamber, Llanallgo, Anglesey, Gwynedd (page 67). OS Map 114 (106) SH 502861 (C).

LOANHEAD OF DAVIOT recumbent stone circle, Old Meldrum, Gordon, Grampian (page 82). OS Map 38 (40), NJ 747288 (HBM-SDD).

LOCH EYRE standing stones, Kenselyre, Trotternish, Isle of Skye (page 109). OS Map 23 (24), NG 414525.

LONG STONE standing stone, Minchinhampton, Gloucestershire (page 177). OS Map 162 (156), ST 884999.

LORDENSHAWS cup-and-ring marks, Rothbury, Northumberland (page 145). OS Map 81 (71), NZ 055993. Beside path to fort.

LUNDIN LINKS standing stones, Largo Bay, Fife (page 166). OS Map 59 (56), NO 404027. Can be seen from the road or permission sought at the Lundin Links Golf Club.

MACHRIE MOOR stone circles, Blackwaterfoot, Isle of Arran (pages 57, 92, 93). OS Map 69 (66), NR 910324 and area (HBM-SDD).

MAEN Y BARDD burial chamber, Rhiw, Roewen, Conwy Valley, Gwynedd (page 158). OS Map 115 (107), SH 740718.

MAES HOWE chambered cairn, Tormiston, Orkney Mainland (page 125). OS Map 6 (6), HY 318127 (HBM-SDD). Restricted opening hours and admission charge.

MAYBURGH Henge, Penrith, Cumbria (page 100). OS Map 90 (83), NY 519285 (EH).

MEN-AN-TOL holed stone, Morvah, West Penwith, Cornwall (page 153). OS Map 203 (189), SW 427349.

MEN GURTA standing stone, St Breock Down, Bodmin, Cornwall (page 143). OS Map 200 (185), SW 967683 (EH).

MERRIVALE stone rows, Dartmoor, Devon (page 115). OS Map 191 (187), SX 553746 (EH).

MIDMAR KIRK recumbent stone circle, Echt, Gordon, Grampian (page 121). OS Map 68 (40), NJ 699064.

MINNINGLOW HILL megalithic cists, Parwich, Derbyshire (page 87). OS Map 119 (111), SK 209573. This site is on private land with no right of way; it can be seen, but not visited, from the Roystone Grange archaeological trail.

MULFRA QUOIT, West Penwith, Cornwall (back cover). OS Map 203 (189), SW 452354.

NETHER LARGIE NORTH cairn, Kilmartin Valley, Argyll (pages 136–7). OS Map 55 (52), NR 832985 (HBM-SDD).

NEWBIGGIN cup-and-ring marked stone, Perth and Kinross (page 141). OS Map 53 (49), NO 155352.

NINE MAIDENS stone row, St Columb Major, Bodmin, Cornwall (page 114). OS Map 200 (185), SW 937675.

NINE STONE CLOSE stone circle, Harthill Moor, Birchover, Derbyshire (page 2). OS Map 119 (111), SK 225625.

ORMAIG rock carvings, nr. Kilmartin, Mid Argyll (page 144). OS Map 55 (52), NM 823027.

PENRHOS FEILW standing stones, nr. Holyhead, Anglesey, Gwynedd (page 53). OS Map 114 (106), SH 227809 (C).

QUOYNESS chambered cairn, Sanday, Orkney (pages 11, 37). OS Map 5 (5), HY 676377 (HBM-SDD).

RHIW standing stone, nr. Roewen, Conwy Valley, Gwynedd (page 159). OS Map 115 (107), SH 736716.

RILLATON round barrow and cist, Linkinhorne, Bodmin Moor, Cornwall (page 64). OS Map 201 (186), SX 260719.

RING OF BRODGAR henge and stone circle, Stennes, Orkney Mainland (pages 41, 102, 103). OS Map 6 (6), HY 294134 (HBM-SDD).

THE ROLLRIGHT STONES stone circle, Rollright, Oxfordshire (page 111). OS Map 151(145), SP 296308. Private ownership; a charge may be made.

ROUGHTING LINN cup-and-ring marks, Bar Moor, Lowick, Northumberland (page 130). OS Map 75 (64), NT 984367.

RUDH'AN DUNAIN chambered cairn, Glenbrittle, Isle of Skye (page 71). OS Map 32 (33) NG 393164.

RUDSTON MONOLITH, nr. Bridlington, North Humberside (page 51). OS Map 101 (93), TA 097677.

SHOWERY TOR cairn, Rough Tor, Bodmin Moor, Cornwall (page 56). OS Map 200 (186), SX 149814 (NT).

SILBURY HILL artificial mound, West Kennett, Avebury, Wiltshire (pages 42, 43). OS Map 173 (157), SU 100685 (EH). Car park and viewing area but no access to hill itself.

STANTON DREW stone circles, avenues and cove, Chew Magna, Avon (pages 50, 164). OS Map 172 (166), ST 601634 (EH). Closed Sunday. Access via private land: the owner may levy a charge. Cove in garden of Druid's Arms, ST 598633.

STONES OF STENNES henge and stone circle, Orkney Mainland (page 40, front cover). OS Map 6 (6), HY 306125 (HBM-SDD).

STONEY LITTLETON chambered long barrow, Wellow, Avon (pages 46, 47). OS Map 172 (166) ST 735573 (EH).

SUNHONEY recumbent stone circle, Echt, Gordon, Grampian (page 120). OS Map 38 (40), NJ 715056.

TAVERSÖE TUICK chambered cairn, Trumland, Rousay, Orkney (pages 78, 79). OS Map 6 (6), HY 427276 (HBM-SDD).

THORNBOROUGH (central) henge, West Tanfield, Ripon, North Yorkshire (page 95). OS Map 100 (91), SE 285795.

TORMORE chambered cairn, Blackwaterfoot, Isle of Arran (page 93). OS Map 69 (66), NR 903310.

TRETHEVY QUOIT, St Cleer, Liskeard, Cornwall (page 63). OS Map 201 (186), SX 259688 (EH).

TŶ-MAWR standing stone, Holyhead, Anglesey, Gwynedd (page 142). OS Map 114 (106), SH 254810 (C).

UNIVAL chambered cairn, Kirkibost, North Uist, Outer Hebrides (page 171). OS Map 18 (17), NF 800668.

UNSTAN chambered cairn, Stennes, Orkney Mainland (page 151). OS Map 6 (6), HY 283117 (HBM-SDD). Standard opening hours; key at house beside cairn.

VERYAN round barrow, Carne, nr. St Austell, Cornwall (page 59). OS Map 204 (190), SW 913386.

WAYLAND'S SMITHY chambered long barrow, Uffington, Oxfordshire (page 69). OS Map 174 (158), SU 281854 (EH).

WEST KENNET AVENUE (of standing stones), Avebury, Wiltshire (page 97). OS Map 173 (157), SU 105693 (EH, NT).

WEST KENNET chambered long barrow, Avebury, Wiltshire (page 45). OS Map 173 (157), SU 104677 (EH).

WIDEFORD HILL chambered cairn, nr. Kirkwall, Orkney Mainland (page 74). OS Map 6 (6), HY 409122 (HBM-SDD).

YELLOWMEAD concentric stone circles, nr. Yelverton, Dartmoor, Devon (page 170). OS Map 202 (187), SX 575677.

ZENNOR QUOIT, nr. St. Ives, West Penwith, Cornwall (page 150). OS Map 203 (189), SW 468380.

ACKNOWLEDGEMENTS

Over the years, the following people have aided my photography and understanding of ancient sites by their conversation, practical help and hospitality – Philip Abramson, Lindsay Badenoch, Rosemary and Tony Baker, John Barnatt, Hubert and Monica Beales, John Blakemore, Cilla Boniface, Steve Boyle, Aubrey Burl, Neil Carver, Donna and Phil Cunningham, Tim Darvill, Dave Fine, Peter Fowler, Ann Hammond, Carolyn Heighway, Fleur Howles, Linda and Peter Jeavons, Jim Killgore, Angus and Sadie Lockhart, Dave Longley, Frances Lynch, Pat Lynch, Ann MacSween, John and Rhoda MacSween, Bev Margerison, Richard Morris, Gina and Roger Martlew, Maggie Mason, Frank and Louise Moran, Dave and Paige Morgan, Sue Page, Clive Ruggles, Dave and Julie Sangwine, Alan Saville, Dorothy and Walter Sharp, Roger and Tania Simpson, Chris Smith, Dave Thompson, Jane Timby, Brian Williamson and Kath Williamson.

My thanks to Richard Bryant of Alan Sutton's for giving me the chance to produce this book, and then helping me to make it work. Also to Christopher Chippindale for enhancing my photographs with his deeper understanding of ancient sites and landscapes.

And finally, my particular thanks to Jean Williamson, who has suffered most for my interest in Britain's past, yet done more than anyone to help me pursue it.

Mick Sharp
June 1989